The Marti

The Martial Arts Woman

Andrea Harkins

Library of Congress Cataloging-in-Publication Data
Andrea Harkins, 1963-

The Martial Arts Woman

ISBN-13:978-1544916217

1. Martial Arts. 2. Women. 3. Self-Help. 4. Title

Endorsements for The Martial Arts Woman

This is a much-needed book that is very well executed. The martial arts can appear to be a very masculine affair from the outside (and even from within at times). Testosterone, muscles and two guys beating the living daylights out of each other are the images that leap to mind for most. The martial arts can be much more than that though. They can be an empowering way of life – for men and women alike.

We take the lessons learned in the dojo – lessons in resilience, discipline, commitment, strength and adaptability – and apply them to our lives. Life can be as brutal and challenging as any fight.

Gichin Funakoshi, often called "The Father of Modern Karate," said, "One whose spirit and mental strength have been strengthened by sparring with a never-say-die attitude should find no challenge too great to handle. One who has undergone long years of physical pain and mental agony to learn one punch, one kick, should be able to face any task, no matter how difficult, and carry it through to the end. A person like this can truly be said to have learned karate."

I agree! The contributors to this book have embodied that martial spirit in the tales they share. Their stories and insights also embody a true femininity, a femininity of strength, determination, compassion, insight and power. This is a book written by warrior women and it will inspire all who read it.

As I write this, the love of my life, herself a martial arts woman, is pregnant with our daughter. Our daughter will be educated in the martial arts, because we both want her to be a martial arts woman too. The lessons outlined in this book are exactly the ones we wish to impart to her though the martial arts. It's a joy to read this coming together of martial values, life lessons, and feminine strength. A brilliant book!

Iain Abernethy, 6th Dan in karate

Endorsements for The Martial Arts Woman

This brilliant, heartfelt, and unapologetically honest mosaic of non-fiction, transforms our sense of how deep and profound this topic of the "Martial Arts Woman" is. Andrea's work will undoubtedly impact women now and for generations to come. Real. Affecting. Powerful. Courageous. Entertaining.

Michelle Manu
Senior Black Belt and Kumu in the Kaihewalu Hawaiian Lua

Endorsements for The Martial Arts Woman

The Martial Arts Woman is a collection of short articles and stories that you will find highly motivating and inspirational. This inspiring book demonstrates how the martial arts are about more than self-defense and competition. As you travel the path of the martial arts, you are transformed into a stronger, more confident person; your spirit develops a never-say-die mindset that will give you strength that you never knew you had.

That is what this book is all about! You will read true stories about how these women's martial arts training helped them overcome tremendous odds and overwhelming challenges in their lives. You will be moved as you read how these women strived for victory in life

The women included in this book have demonstrated the martial arts spirit in their lives. Whether you are interested in the martial arts or not, you will find inspiration from these stories of triumph.

Bohdi Sanders 5th degree black belt and author of:
The Warrior Ethos and *Modern Bushido: Living a Life of Excellence*

Endorsements for The Martial Arts Woman

The Martial Arts Woman by Andrea Harkins should be required reading for any person teaching martial arts. I've taught professionally since 1976. My best students, and biggest supporters, were always women.

This book has stories from 24 female black belts on what the martial arts has meant in their lives. I had no idea. This is not a cookie cutter compilation. There are no Bruce Lee or Chuck Norris inspired black belts here.

The inspiration for these women comes from a much deeper, and at times, a much darker place. These are powerful stories that provide an insight that all instructors could benefit from reading. I know I did.

John Graden
The Martial Arts Teacher of Teachers

Endorsements for The Martial Arts Woman

The Martial Arts Woman by Andrea Harkins, is probably the first book written about female martial artists that does not explore training or style, but how women apply martial arts to their lives.

This excellent book reveals an array of stories and insights from 25 martial arts women with a common theme of perseverance and warrior-ship. These personal stories are complemented by chapters about topics that reach back in Andrea's span of 27 years in the arts. Each chapter is independently written which makes it easy to read so you can explore chapters that are interesting to you.

Sensei Andrea explores the spirit and psyche of the martial arts woman from all angles. While training is discussed, the focus of her first book is on how the martial art woman explores the martial arts mindset in her life.

This book is a must read for everyone — both martial and non-martial artists alike. You'll find stories that inspire and motivate you on many different levels. Clearly, it has a direct association with martial art practitioners and instructors. Beyond that, these stories will inspire everyone because they are about life's lessons, motivation, and turning overwhelming difficulties into Triumphs. Highly recommended!

Grandmaster Andrew S. Linick, Hanshi
10th Dan and publisher of Official Karate Magazine

Endorsements for The Martial Arts Woman

Andrea Harkins has put together a martial arts book that every follower of the martial ways should read. Although her work is woman-centric, there are lessons for everyone who trains, or has trained in the martial arts.

The work is inspirational, thought provoking, and tearfully telling of female pioneers that paved the way for other women to enjoy the benefits of the modern martial arts school.

Grab this book, read it, ingest it, deeply consider it, then smile knowing that you've taken part in something amazing. These incredible women have poured out their hearts; at the very least, we should all appreciate their stories!

Howard Upton
Author of: *Of Blood and Stone* and *Occam's Razor*

Endorsements for The Martial Arts Woman

Congratulations to Sensei Andrea Harkins on this great and important work! While inspiring and educational, this book is a must read for all martial artists, men, women, and children alike.

Featuring several of my own martial arts heroes, this book challenges you to see the arts through another's eyes and understand that training can mean different things to each individual. It is entertaining and packed with wisdom. Enjoy!

Kevin Bergquist
Author, Actor, 3-time Karate State Champion
Guinness World Records Concrete Breaker

Endorsements for The Martial Arts Woman

The Martial Arts Woman is an easy-to-read, feel-good book featuring short stories of women from many walks of life who have chosen to embark on a "martial journey" to self-improvement. In this book, you will learn far more than discipline and defense; you will discover how each used the arts to catapult them to goal achievement, empowerment, self-healing, motivation, to overcome would-be obstacles, and to skyrocket their self-confidence and sense of well-being.

Caution! This book may cause you to feel extreme inspiration and admiration for those who have shared their stories.

Kathy Marlor Kozlowski
Owner St. Pete Self Defense, 4th degree black belt & former world champion

Endorsements for The Martial Arts Woman

I love the different "personalities" and writing styles of all the gals in this book! Reading it gave me an opportunity get to know where they are coming from. I also really like how your own thoughts intermingle between the chapters. This book has a great flow!

Restita DeJesus
Teacher of Tai Chi, Wushu, Filipino Martial Arts,
and Kung Fu at Seattle Wushu Center

Endorsements for The Martial Arts Woman

The Martial Arts Woman is a unique entry in the landscape of martial arts books. The depth of stories are varied and not just about martial arts, but about the impact martial arts can have on life.

This book is inspirational, articulate and engaging. *The Martial Arts Woman* is a well-written book that everyone, regardless of gender or affiliation to any particular martial art, should read.

Jeremy Lesniak
Founder Whistlekick, LLC

Endorsements for The Martial Arts Woman

With all of the martial arts related books that come out each year, none has approached the topic of women warriors the way that this book does. Throughout history, women warriors have defended themselves, their families and even their homelands against the most dangerous attackers. Now we get to see these many battles through the eyes of those who lived it in our modern time.

These are stories of women who have been empowered by the strength that martial arts training gives you, both physically and mentally. We hear how they developed confidence while facing their own personal struggles. We also, see how they are grateful for how martial arts life lessons made them better people. These women destroy the myth that learning martial arts would make you less feminine.

Men and women alike will share their feelings about how sparring helped them learn to fight life's problems, along with their adversaries. We learn from these stories that courage comes in all shapes and sizes.

The women in this book are positive examples of what wonders can be achieved through the total mind, body and spirit aspects of learning the military arts. What I admire the most about their stories is that these aren't women who showed up to prove something. They showed up to improve something. We can all learn from their examples.

Richard Hackworth
Publisher of *World Martial Arts Magazine*

Acknowledgments

I want to express my sincere appreciation to my husband, David, for his support and help during the many hours I spent writing this book. I would have never been able to do it without him. I would also like to thank my children, Ian, Kevin, Shane and Katie, my mother, and my family who provided encouragement and kind words along the way.

Thank you to my blog readers, co-workers, workout friends, social media connections, martial art students, and my friends who have supported me. For those who have graciously read and reviewed my book prior to publication, thank you. I also thank Brian Malfant, and his assistant, Carlos Maldonado, for my publicity photos during the past year.

I extend a personal thank you to Karen Eden Herdman, who not only contributed chapters to this book and wrote the foreword, but who also became a friend and martial art sister along this journey.

To Joy Turberville, I say thank you for comprehensively illuminating what it means to be a martial art woman. Many who could otherwise never have the chance to understand martial arts from the fascinating and intricate perspective that you provided, will enjoy your chapter.

To each woman who contributed thoughts, stories, insights, quotes, or chapters to this book, I applaud and thank you. There was no trepidation in sharing your stories. Your insights reveal what it means to be a martial arts woman in today's world.

Finally, to you, the reader and purchaser of this book, somewhere in these pages, you will connect with a woman whose essence means something to you. You will stumble upon a chapter where the words leap off the page and into your heart. That is when I will accomplish my goal. Thank you for reading, sharing, and enjoying.

Book Contributors

I would also like to thank the martial arts women who contributed to my book. Each of these ladies opened their hearts and their lives to inspire you with their stories of perseverance and triumph. Thank you all very much!

Alexandra Allred
Colleen Davis
Colleen Diemer
Dana Hee
Dana Stamos
Devorah Yoshiko Dometrich
Jackie Bradbury
Janice Bishop
Jennifer Linch
Jenny Sikora
Jill Diamond Chastain
Joy Turberville
Karen Eden Herdman
Kelina Cowell
Kristin Miller
Lynda Hatch
Marci Faustini
Mary Moonen
Kim Tran
Michelle Manu
Pam Darty
Pam Neil
Patricia Roth
Penny Pitassi
Reese Balliet
Restita DeJesus
Sama Bellomo
Rita Rose Pasquale
Wendy Puffenburger

Table of Contents

Foreword

After 26 years of teaching and training in martial arts, I have this "martial arts woman" thing down pretty well. Honestly, I never even thought of myself as a female student at all, until I had a baby.

That was a pivotal point in my martial art career. It was a point when I realized that I was not like any ordinary male student. I was super human, and stronger than I ever thought I could be. I delivered my baby less than two days after I taught my last class. I went back to teach five days later, and was scheduled to test for the rank of Master in just a few short weeks.

My male counterparts were astounded that I was back and training so quickly, but I did not want anyone to cut me any breaks. I wanted to be able to walk away saying that I exerted the exact amount of sweat, and earned the exact Master's belt, as everyone else. I am a woman and not a victim of circumstances.

My martial art sister, Andrea, is sharing in this theme in her book. It is not about being a victim, but about being a female warrior in training. It is about realizing that you are capable of so much more in life because of your training.

We women took on a role that was male dominated up until the last three or four decades. The men, bless their hearts, really did not know how to take us at first. They would ponder. "Do I hit them just as hard? Do I avoid their chest area?"

Even today, many male students do not like the thought of having to fight a woman, regardless of her rank. That does not offend me. I rather appreciate the respect. But I cannot be the best that I can be if someone else is holding back, male or female.

In this book, there are many battlegrounds. Their health, their past, and their own lives challenged these martial arts women. Learning to master one's self is a journey on which all martial artists will eventually find themselves. It is about discovering who you are and improving confidence, despite the incredible criticism that women often endure, sometimes just because they are women.

The day I taught my first class as a black belt instructor was the hardest class I ever had to teach. All the men were staring at me with doubt and criticism. When I was done many of them needed oxygen, but my male counterparts never disrespected me again.

People often ask me about choosing such a "manly" sport. That is when I show them my pink fingernails and talk about my favorite high-heeled shoes. I love being a woman in every sense of the word. I loved the feeling of testing with the guys, for the rank of master, but I also loved going home and breastfeeding my baby. If I can do that, is there anything I cannot do?

There is nothing in the world stronger than a female martial artist. We are sisters, bound by our incredible "I can" attitude."

Master Karen Eden Herdman
6th Dan Tang Soo Do
Columnist, Book Author

Introduction

A martial arts woman is inspired and motivated by her training. She has nothing to prove, except to herself. Her martial art combines femininity and strength with vulnerability and heroism. This unique and intangible force touches every aspect of her life.

When you think of a woman who practices martial arts, what comes to mind? Do you envision a woman who is a risk-taker and a high achiever, or a woman who does not let obstacles stand in her way? Is she a fighter or a defender? She fits many categories and roles, such as mother, sister, daughter, and best friend.

The martial arts woman knows what she wants. She gives 100% effort, reaches expectations, creates strong and specific goals, and never lets the words, "I can't," stand in her way. Above all, she is a role model, and is admired and respected for her desire to learn a tradition that was once, not all that long ago, forbidden to her.

She fascinates men and women alike because she is an extraordinary woman. I know about the character of the martial arts woman because I am one. My own journey is not unlike the journey of many other women, who have dared to establish themselves as martial artists in a mostly male dominated environment.

I did not know on my first day of martial arts class twenty-seven years ago, that I was about to undergo a magnificent and incredible transformation. Through my martial art training, I gradually changed every falsity, negativity, and presumption that I ever had about myself. This is the power of a martial art woman. It is an awakening to the fact that she is so much more than she ever realized.

Today, women are emerging as fighters in major venues, when in the past only very few women were respected as fighters. This genre of the martial arts woman consists of a fierce determination. They push through boundaries and reach the unexpected. They are our future.

I almost walked away from the dojo after my first class. Watching students perform falls, yells, breaks, and complicated choreographed martial art moves was overwhelming to me. I sat on the gymnasium floor, with dust and dirt swirling around me, and wondered if I was brave enough. As sweat dripped off my back, I listened intently to the deeply controlled yells that erupted around me, and questioned everything about myself.

I worried if I could overcome my own inadequacies to learn what was required. Previously, I turned away many opportunities for self-discovery that came my way because of my lack of self-confidence. I did not start training to prove anything to anyone or to show that as a woman I could master it. My first step was all about finding the real me.

Something happened in the next few classes that engaged my martial art spirit. It was as if I transformed from average me into a different woman. It took a few more classes for me to recognize that I could pour my experiences as a woman into the contemplative and explosive aspects of a fighting art. I found a part of me that I never even knew existed. I found the martial arts woman.

Since that time, I have gained an understanding that comes from years of practicing and teaching. The mindset of any beginner martial artist is specific and guided. The mindset of an experienced female martial artist, however, is unusual and coveted. She is a rare gem.

My journey, and the journeys of so many other women, is worth sharing and documenting for many reasons. Their stories, wisdom, and anecdotes can benefit everyone interested in implementing a strong and courageous martial art mindset in their own lives.

Each chapter in this book is an independent story, so choose to read whatever chapters interest you first. In whatever manner you choose to read this book, be prepared to experience the spirit and psyche of the martial arts woman.

Andrea Harkins

The Martial Arts Woman

Andrea Harkins

MINDSET

Never, never, never,
Never give up.
Winston Churchill

Built of Steel
Andrea Harkins

I wanted to begin this book with a story about a woman who used a martial art mindset to overcome an unexpected, long-term obstacle. I love this story because it shows how a woman persevered and found hope, when others might have given up.

This is the story of a woman who found herself in a situation she never expected. She felt lost and stuck for years. As her world became less stable, she continued to utilize her martial art experiences and mindset to remain centered and balanced. She had no choice, except to pull the frayed, loose strings of this situation together.

This modern martial art woman faced a very unmodern situation, which, in the end, made her a better person. There is a twist or two that explains everything, who this martial art woman is, and why she did what she did. This story is about how her life changed without warning and how, with little resources or energy, she fought her way through it.

This woman, a mother, moved with her family from a small city to a rural area. She and her husband wanted a better environment in which to raise their kids. Mother was patient and creative, and Father was a hard worker.

Mother and Father shared four beautiful children and a background in martial arts. In fact, they taught martial arts together for years and had a great belief in living a martial art way of life. They thought that their martial art mindset would carry them through anything, until they found themselves facing such a difficult situation, that it made them question everything that they ever believed.

The family bought five acres of land in a small rural town. During this time, there was a big boom in the real estate market, and they were unable to find a building contractor. The only way they could move to the acreage was to build the house themselves. They purchased a two story, steel kit home that they could partially erect themselves, and complete with the help of subcontractors.

The steel kit house was much like a large scaled version of a toy erector set, with huge pieces of metal. Big red iron shafts and beams that looked like a stack of metal building blocks were delivered and piled in the backyard. The family predicted a year to build the kit. The yearlong building adventure went awry, and that is what forced Mother to push her martial art mindset and perseverance to the forefront.

Mother had been a martial artist for quite a while. She started practicing long before her house building years. During the construction phase, she struggled to find the time to continue to learn and practice her martial art. Hiring local contractors to pour concrete and erect the home took up a lot of her time and the family's resources.

Martial arts were on hold because of this metal conglomeration of beams and trusses that they needed to erect. Mother's energy for her practice waned. Everything in her life felt slightly out of control, as the one-year building project stretched past two, three, four years, and into five years.

During construction, the steel kit house looked just like other commercial buildings. Steel beams held it together from all angles. The roof was uplifted with big rafters made of heavy red iron. There were two floors, five bedrooms, and 2.5 baths planned.

Through all of this, Mother's martial thoughts were always in the back of her mind. She would turn to them often, along with her faith, to validate what was happening. Martial arts represented hope, and they meant everything to her. This house project was far from what she ever planned or imagined, and she needed to rely on that which she knew and trusted. Her martial art and her martial art mindset had never let her down before.

The family hired some local hands to erect the exterior of the structure and raise the roof. When they moved from the city to the rural acreage, the exterior shell of the steel kit was together. They packed their belongings into storage, and drove to their new, unfinished home.

The truth is there was nowhere else to go. Mother would have to summon her martial art mindset to get through this ordeal, but she did not know for how long.

When Mother, Father, and their four children moved in, there were two large floors of living space with no divisions, no interior walls, and no interior drywall. Like a skeleton, there were metal studs and beams visible throughout. There was no kitchen, no bathroom, no running water, and no electricity.

Living this way was like being a warrior or a pioneer from a different time. The family carried big, chunky flashlights through the house when it was dark. Eventually, a generator was purchased, a generator that they used sparingly, because gas at the time was so expensive. They did not need much electricity anyway. They spent a lot of time outside, and everyone went to bed at around 9:00 p.m. each night.

During the few hours, when the generator ran, the kids played video games or watched television. Their parents washed the laundry and hung their clothes on a clothesline outside. Because the children were home schooled, they used most of their time to explore around the small pond out front or the mound of fill dirt. They did not realize that they were living any differently than anyone else, but Mother knew it was different and maybe even unacceptable to many. She pushed it to the back of her mind.

Mother, Father, and all the kids slept together in one big room on the second floor. At first, there was nothing to divide the space. Eventually they hung the drywall and revealed some bedrooms.

They constructed a picnic table downstairs where they ate meals together, or played cards and board games. There was no kitchen, but there were planks of plywood that made makeshift counters. They could use a toaster or a microwave on occasion, but Father cooked almost all the meals on a propane grill in the back yard.

They took showers in the back yard with a water hose. The kids were young and did not really care much that they were showering out in the open. The property was big, and there was no chance that anyone could see them. Living this way was a lot like camping. In the evenings, they could always see a big expansive starlit sky. When it was night and quiet, it was easy to see every star in the sky.

The evening was the only time when Mother's martial art mind was at ease and clear. She tried to control the worry and the fear, but it stayed very close to the surface. She knew that they could lose everything if they did not figure out how to finish building the house.

When everyone was asleep, she would sit quietly and visualize her katas and think of her strengths. She would recall the times when she struggled in her practice, but overcame, and the times when she was unsteady, but still pushed through. She broke boards and barriers in martial arts, even when she was unsure of herself. This was not much different.

Mother would meditate and seek hope, even though she knew that the family was living so primitively. They could have just as easily been in a tent in the woods somewhere, except this structure had exterior walls and a roof.

During the week, Mother continued to work at her professional job. On her daily one-hour commute, she would think of a couple of things. One was her martial art, and the other was her self-confidence. She wondered how she could face her boss and co-workers without feeling like a failure, or letting on that she was stuck in a situation that was seemingly out of control.

At times, she felt her black belt perseverance waning. If her martial art could not see her through here, she knew it would be lost forever. Before stepping into work in the morning, she took a big, martial art kind of breath, exhaled slowly, and went inside. She never told anyone about the big building project that consumed her life outside of work. She looked like everyone else, with her makeup and professional clothes.

There was no one with whom she could share this experience. People would think that she was crazy for living in this mess. They would never understand that she did not have any money left, or that contractors walked away, or took other jobs, when she needed their help the most. Even today, it is difficult for her to explain her situation to others.

No one knew that every morning she would sit in her car at home, (because turning on the generator required a trek into the overgrown backyard), and put her makeup on, while staring into the car mirror. She saw herself staring back and often asked herself how many years would she be showering in the back yard or putting makeup on in the car.

She reached her breaking point many times, but fought back. She knew that one day the house would be finished, and she would return to being a normal person and martial artist again. She just did not know when. Looking back, she never was more of a martial artist than she was during those years.

It is ironic that it had taken her five long years to earn her black belt, and that it also took five long years living in the unfinished house with her family before it was finished. She lived like this through cold, wet Florida winters, and hot, humid summers with no air conditioning.

During the chilly winter nights, the family slept in sleeping bags and sometimes sported knit caps before turning in. The summers were the opposite and even worse. It was so stifling hot that they opened all the windows and took outdoor showers to stay cool. Now, when the family hears someone complain about air conditioning not working for a one single night, they look at each other with a smile.

There were also many unexpected guests in the unfinished house. A group of baby skunks buried their way under the downstairs bathroom shower. Father had to get a humane trap to remove them. He covered the trap with a big square cloth so the skunks would not spray him when he carried the trap outside.

On occasion, a snake would make an appearance. There were even venomous snakes, like water moccasins and rattlesnakes. Mother and her family learned to keep each other safe, to lookout for the unexpected guests.

During the commotion of building the house, and dealing with the critters, Mother continued to turn to her martial art mindset. If she did not, everything would fall apart. She had to be strong enough to face the few people who did know about the project, because they provided little encouragement.

The naysayers did not believe that the family could complete such a huge effort, but the family believed. Still, they had some rough patches. On occasion, they took turns wanting to walk away from it, but they always worked it out. That was martial arts perseverance. They relied upon it. If anything, they learned how to bond together and, occasionally do without. They knew what they needed. It was plain and simple. They needed each other.

One day, after five long years of hard work, they finally completed the big, two-story, steel kit home. It had a full porch upstairs and plenty of comfortable space. They did not have to use a propane grill to cook anymore. There was a big kitchen. They stopped taking showers outside, and no longer needed to run a generator for electricity.

They had literally camped for five years, and stretched the funds from the construction loan as far as they could. The bank ceased pressuring them and there were no more threats about foreclosure Naysayers fell by the wayside. Mother never had to stare in the car mirror to apply her makeup ever again. They packed the flashlights away. There was need to worry or hide the truth anymore. Everyone could move forward with life.

This is such an inspiring story of overcoming an unexpected obstacle. I could not have told it any better than if I had lived it myself. The truth is that I did live it. I am Mother in this story, and it is my personal testimony of using my martial art mindset in an incredibly difficult time in my life.

The decision to build the steel kit home was not easy. We needed a bigger home, and this was a less costly solution than traditional home building. We never expected it to take five years. Many setbacks happened during that time. There were concrete shortages, drywall shortages, and the late issuance of a building permit. It was difficult to find workers who were not already busy working on other building projects.

Everything worked against us, and we found ourselves having to complete most of the work ourselves, from hanging drywall, to installing electrical work, plumbing fixtures, and painting. The most surprising part is that it all finally fell into place with just the hands and hearts of Mother, Father, and four small children. This is where my sense of perseverance comes, and why I find inspiration and motivation in the smallest of life's moments. I learned it all from living in an unfinished house for five years.

We built something else together as a family. Not long after finishing the house, we started a martial art program at the local YMCA. Building a good martial art program is like building a steel house. It takes hard work, patience, and the desire to make it work.

Because of my martial art philosophies and unique life experiences, I know I can overcome any obstacle. I can thank two different five-year stints in my life for that, earning a black belt and building a house. I did not give up, because I could not. I could not sell a half-finished house, and I did not have the money or options to buy another one. When you have no options or other viable choices, you do what you must, and in the end, you are better for it.

Many people are not willing to sacrifice as much as we did to create the life they really want. Our goal was to raise our four children in a place where they could thrive. The construction took an unexpected five years, and ranks up there with one of the most difficult endeavors I have ever faced. But I can honestly say that I am a better person because of it. Lives made of steel are different. They can withstand any storm.

A life lesson clearly emerges. What is in your house? Certainly, life has thrown curve balls your way and you have had to face challenges or make difficult choices. All I can tell you is that it is impossible to determine exactly what will happen in your life. You make decisions, do the best you can, and hope that it turns out well. Your life, like my steel-kit house, is waiting to be constructed. Plan on how you want to put it all together, and build upon it. Be ready to work for it.

If you ever seriously ask yourself if you can finish what you have started, or if you want to quit because the task is too difficult, I have one thing to say to you after struggling through these difficult moments of my life – I learned how to succeed. You can too!

Life is either a daring Adventure or nothing.
Helen Keller

Do not fear challenges, embrace them. When you face them, and find a way to resolve them, you will find peace within.

Andrea Harkins
"The Martial Arts Woman"

The Empowered Woman
Andrea Harkins

The martial arts woman sees the world differently than most people. She becomes more self-assured and starts to eliminate the fear or low self-esteem that hindered her in the past, because her physicality and mentality combine. As she learns what empowerment means in her life, others are already in the process of making their own assumptions about her. They see her as an ordinary person, until they learn that she is a martial artist.

When I tell someone that I practice martial arts, it is as if I transform right in front of their eyes from a regular woman, to a woman worth special attention. I am suddenly far more intriguing. The image of the martial arts woman conjures up thoughts of strength and power.

When I was posing for some photographs recently, I realized the impact that being a female martial artist has on others. The photographer and his assistant first took some photographs of me in my regular clothes. Then, I changed into my uniform.

My demeanor also changed. I was no longer the professional and friendly woman they had seen moments earlier. I looked more serious. I stretched quietly and tied my belt in silence. Although I had no desire to impress them, I was impressionable by my martial art.

An online dictionary describes the word, "empowerment," to make someone stronger and more confident, especially in controlling their life and claiming their rights. For women in martial arts, this concept is very true. Through martial arts, women begin to achieve that which they thought was impossible.

Sparring, yelling, breaking, breathing, controlling, focusing, and increasing awareness all become part of her empowerment and strength. Many women learn how to be friendly, thoughtful, generous, and kind, but have never learned how to yell, kick, punch, or defend. Martial arts empower them to break through these mental and physical barriers.

Female practitioners recognize that they are not vulnerable. Many share testimonies about how martial arts have improved their physical and mental defenses. Rather than describing themselves as vulnerable, they start to see themselves as determined and dedicated.

On a moment's notice, a martial arts woman must go from perceived vulnerability to a fighting mentality and fierce determination. She must learn to quickly recognize and address dangerous situations and encounters. Her training directly affects how quickly she acts and reacts.

Not long ago, a fire broke out in my backyard. I heard some commotion, and when I looked out the upstairs window, I could see a fire engulfing the backyard like a big ring expanding closer and closer to the house (yes, the house that took us five years to build!).

My husband and children were already outside by the time I realized what was happening. There was no time to make a call, to prepare myself, or to figure out exactly what was going on. Fire needs no explanation. If you do not proceed swiftly, precious time is lost.

I ran downstairs and filled buckets of water from a big laundry sink inside. Running back and forth from one side of the fire to the other, I tried to stop it from expanding. My family sprayed the fire with water hoses. I had no time to think about what I was doing. I simply took immediate action. I needed to apply this instantaneous type of response that I learned from martial arts training.

How many times had I struggled to remember the right steps in a kata or the correct placement of my foot for a kick? How long had I waited for the right amount of strength and power to develop, so I could react without thinking?

Throughout the years, I rehearsed the same monotonous and repetitive techniques repeatedly. All that practice gave me the strength to fight real fires, and to battle mental fires too. Empowerment does not always have such a devastating impact as a raging fire. It can present itself subtly, like an aura that felt more than seen. It happens after years of practice. Either way, the martial art woman must always be prepared.

Everyone has a vision of who the martial arts woman is. Her empowerment naturally builds throughout her life, and she stores it within until she needs to use it. There is no need to flaunt it because its authenticity is apparent. Whatever situations affect the martial art woman in her lifetime, whether fires, difficult decisions, or an unexpected need for defense, she will learn to face it and embrace it with empowerment.

The Female Ninja Prophecy
Andrea Harkins

A martial art woman is partially a ninja at heart. She may not realize it, but she is destined to fill that prophecy. Her ninja-like conscience and spirit naturally strengthen over time because of her martial art practice and training. She will likely face some type of battle in her lifetime, and that is when she will first discover it.

Some ninja enthusiasts describe a ninja as a covert agent, whose functions include things like espionage, sabotage, open combat, and war. This seems far-fetched in modern times and not a very accurate description of a female martial artist. Today's version of the ninja, however, is in a positive light and portrayed as an action hero, acrobat, karate expert, and even a turtle.

How can a martial art woman fit in that mix? She must toggle her responsibilities, commitments, and womanhood with the tenets of a fighting art, as she evolves into ninja-like status.

Should she throw everything she has learned about being a woman out the window? Is learning to be combative the same as being defensive, diligent, and responsible? Does learning a martial art imply that a woman will put up her fists and fight, if she must?

The martial art woman understands that she is not exempt from difficulties, and she may need to fight back, either mentally or physically, depending on the circumstances. She can combat it effectively in a ninja-warrior way, utilizing the martial art tools in her arsenal and her martial art mindset.

Like a ninja in martial art class, a woman may learn self-defense against attackers, with and without weapons. She understands that in one wrong turn of events, she may need to defend herself. This awareness is paramount in her training. Even more important is how she copes with the situation at hand.

Have you ever had a gun thrust against your back or aimed at your head? In some cases, there is no defense. When someone is standing several feet away, there is no way to block, deflect, or disengage it.

Recently, a friend shared a story with me. Someone shot her cousin twice in the head with a rifle. Her cousin survived, but remembers every moment. The attacker was standing several feet away from her, aimed, and shot her. There was nothing physically that she could do to prevent it or defend against it. Now, she is engaged in a battle for survival.

She must apply the ninja warrior mindset rapidly. She must believe that she can fight back, and in doing so, has a chance for survival. A woman placed in this predicament has only two choices, to give up or to engage the ninja prophecy that is deep inside.

Can a woman trained as a martial artist absolutely save her life, even in the direst of circumstances? Unfortunately, no. There are no guarantees because there are so many different scenarios that can happen. She must view defense the same way the ninja thinks about scaling a wall. She must learn how to develop her balance and how to pull herself up and over the barriers using reaction and intuition while not knowing what is on the other side.

A new martial artist does not grasp all of this. She only understands bits and pieces. For the most part, she thinks a martial art is a physical activity and a defense system, but she does not realize that through her training, she will develop a ninja warrior mindset.

A martial art woman will learn to battle fully, when necessary. If you told this prophecy to a woman on her first day of martial art class, she would be concerned and wonder if she should hightail it back home. That is why the female ninja prophecy reveals slowly while a woman acclimates to her art. She will grow into it.

The female martial artist will fulfill her mission in many ways. There will always be a mental or physical struggle that she must face. It may not be a gunshot, or some twisted espionage, but she will face her share of difficulties, and she will need a strong mindset to overcome them.

Most importantly, she must believe that if something dangerous or unexpected comes her way, she has the tools needed to manipulate the situation in her favor. She knows, deep down, that she must call upon her ninja prophecy to quickly and efficiently keep everything under control.

Many believe ninjas were not very nice. They think that they were devious, or even evil. While all of that may be true, I would like to think that they had some good attributes from which we can all learn. Many female martial artists will assume the ninja-like status and implement it in their lives.

Applying this prophecy is not something a woman particularly wants or understands, but it is part of her maturation as a martial artist. She may never realize its potential until she must use it. Deep within, in the background of her training, the prophecy steadily grows so she can defend herself or save others when faced with danger.

Mediocre
Karen Eden Herdman

Girls are tough on each other. I recently asked a good friend of mine, "Why would another woman not like me when she doesn't even know me?" She replied, "Because you seem like you are so together and have no problems. It's kind of annoying." I spent some time pondering her comments.

By no means have I had an easy journey on this path called life. I feel sure that my life has been much harder than most. In my early adulthood, I often wondered why some people had every event, every step, and every detail fall right into place, when I was walking alone in the dark, praying that my feet would lead me in the right direction.

I think I have finally figured it out. Those who have a mediocre life, also have a mediocre pay off. That is not necessarily a bad thing, but there are some of us not designed to live a mediocre life.

Those who have never trained in martial arts may think that someone who trained was essentially in control of her life. As an instructor, I know that nothing could be farther from the truth. I can hardly think of one student who has no challenge in her own journey in some way. The difference is that these students muster up the discipline to show up for class and train.

Sometimes, it is a sacrifice. Sometimes, you do not feel like leaving the house when life gets tough. The beauty of martial arts is that if you apply yourself, even if you do not feel like it, you will learn that there is no impossible journey.

On many occasions, I have told my young students, "Your Sabomnim (Master) didn't have an easy life, but she is where she is today, not because she did everything right, but because she never quit trying."

It is true. I did not step in the right direction 100% of the time, but I never stopped putting one foot in front of the other when things got scary either. Even if I had to stop momentarily, and take the slowest calculated step of my life, it was still a step.

To this day, when I wake up, I remind myself that the day should not be mediocre. I face the day like a warrior and embrace whatever may be in my path. I must let go and trust that the God-given system put in place will work for me. I must trust and believe God hears my prayers. My journey is a way to make a difference in the lives of other people.

I have discovered that those in my path should be there and vice versa. Ninety-nine percent of the time, we are meant to tell each other, "Don't worry if your life seems to be out of order right now; that is why our paths crossed. It's not because you're a failure, it's because you were not meant to be mediocre."

Perception is a powerful tool.
Shannon Lee

VALIDATION

I'm not in this world to live up to your expectations, and you are not in this world to live up to mine.
Bruce Lee

Validation
Andrea Harkins

Every woman has a different reason for learning a martial art. I validate every reason, whether it is for fitness, health, exercise, creativity, self-empowerment, confidence, or personal fulfillment. Some martial artists think that these are not worthy goals, but I disagree.

To me, a woman's initial reasoning does not matter, because one day her martial art experience will become something much more important than she ever realized. She will no longer need anyone's validation.

When I began learning martial arts, I had no goals in mind, other than to learn something new. Over time, my goals changed. Instead of wanting to learn something new, I wanted to learn to live a happier, healthier life, using a positive martial art mindset. As an instructor, I do not care what my students' reasons are for learning. I know that in the end, the goal will morph into exactly what they need.

For every new student, tackling a martial art is very like learning a foreign language. At first, it does not make sense. It is difficult and somewhat frustrating to grasp all the concepts, protocols, and techniques. The instructor may speak in the native language of the art. It takes years for the student to become fluent.

Fitness may be a woman's initial goal, but she will eventually notice that martial arts serve other purposes as well, and that they far outweigh general fitness. While they include a hearty dose of aerobic warm-ups, stretches, and self-defense, they are so much more than that. Martial arts are the language of tradition, skill, and power.

Some women find it difficult to decide to learn a martial art because they have a small fear about what martial arts really are. The nature of self-defense sounds scary, violent, and physical. No woman likes the idea of gouging someone's eyes out or doing whatever it takes to escape, but in real life, it could be unavoidable.

Because of this, it is difficult to convince some women to take classes or learn self-defense. They do not think that they are capable of the physically demanding skills that may be expected, and often have misconceptions and anxieties about them. I have advertised self-defense classes for women, and I have priced them reasonably, but women do not sign up. The fear of the unknown or the lack of quality information about martial arts or self-defense deters their attendance. For some, they do not know what to expect, so they will not try.

A woman needs to find a self-defense or martial art program that responds to her personality, needs, fears, and concerns. The question instructors and school owners always should ask themselves is how to get more women to walk through the door. Each woman can benefit from martial arts and self-defense, so we need to help them eliminate the fear. How can we alleviate this worry? How can more women be convinced that they have an inner strength that they have yet to discover? How can they be convinced that self-defense is important?

Providing clear descriptions about what happens in classes might help. Having a female instructor, for some, may be a decision factor. Hearing from other women who are practicing or have attended classes may give some comfort, too.

For these reasons, I will always substantiate a woman's reason for learning a martial art, no matter what it is. Fitness, health, or weight issues are just as good reasons to start as any. No matter what the starting point, training will eventually respond to her needs and give her the benefits of defense and self-protection.

I can see how I would have been much safer in my own life if I had trained earlier. I recall a situation in my teens when I felt scared and vulnerable, but had no recourse. If I had then, even a small amount of the physical and mental self-defense training that I have now, I would have controlled the situation better.

I was a young teenager and out with a group of girls and boys at a social event. The person who was going to give me a ride home unexpectedly went home. Another adult chaperone picked a teenage boy to drive my friend home and me instead. I did not know him.

At the chaperone's prompting, we went with him. He turned out to be a mean bully. He had a knife in his car trunk and threatened that he would harm us if we told anyone about it. I was very happy when I made it home safely.

This incident appears mild compared to some of the women I know. One woman was walking alone when a car pulled up beside her. She had to run to get away. Another woman was jogging in the early morning and resorted to hiding behind bushes in her neighborhood as the car circled the area looking for her. No woman wants to find herself in these types of situations, but they happen.

There is no foolproof defense, even if you train. Exposure is limited, but not eliminated. I did some research to learn more about abductions, and what the victim did that caused her to fall prey to a perpetrator. I located some very simple scenarios that were precursors to highly publicized abductions, some of which lasted for many years.

An 11-year-old girl was walking from her house to a bus stop, a car slowed down. Thinking the driver was going to ask for directions, she walked up to the car.

A 20-year-old woman accepted a ride to attend a friend's birthday party. Even though hitchhiking was unsafe, she still got into their car because the young couple inside appeared clean cut and had their baby with them.

You may read these and think that you, or someone you know, would make the same choices. These are examples of what not to do. None of these victims used awareness. None considered that they did not need to talk to a stranger, even if they appeared to need help or had a baby with them. They completely compromised their awareness because they were kind and wanted to help.

When I had the scary encounter with the boy tasked with driving me home, I could have done a few things better. I could have been more aware and noticed he was agitated. I could have used some verbal de-escalation techniques. I could have turned around and walked away. As women, we learn to be polite and to follow instructions, but we do not always understand that if something does not feel right that we should listen to our intuition.

I got into that boy's car; that was the mistake. Lucky for me, his temper did not warrant me having to defend myself, but even if I had to, I was not prepared. He could have easily overpowered me. I had no experience fighting back, or escaping from a larger sized person.

Therefore, having a male partner in class is a good idea. Training with a larger sized person allows a woman to feel the strength of larger arms around her, or the grip of hands that are twice the size of hers. As she explores self-defense skills, she can rehearse the defenses that work best for her.

One of the drills that I use to help students practice their self-defense techniques in class is called "four corners." There are many variations to this game, but four students of various sizes stand in the corners. One student enters and stands in the center using an attention stance. The students in the corners take turns "attacking" the student in the center of the ring.

One by one, they quickly run in to grab her. It is a great test of defense because reactions must be swift. The defender confirms her strengths, but also learns weaknesses.

Martial arts allow a woman to explore unsafe scenarios in a safe setting. Good awareness can show how it might prevent her from an attack in the first place. A woman may never encounter a person whose judgment is misguided, jumbled, or uncontrolled. If she does, she must reconsider the nice, kind, and respectful way that she normally acts.

A woman who practices a martial art has a lot on her mind and may not initially recognize the changes taking place. Unknowingly, on that first day of class, when she thinks she is pursuing this goal for fitness or self-confidence, she also begins to equip herself with skills that can save her life. Once she figures out the truth about what martial arts can do for her, she will never worry about or seek validation again.

Life is not about finding yourself. Life is about creating yourself.
Lolly Daskal

Finding Confidence
Reese Balliet

I am sixteen-years old. Even at my age, I have had to apply a martial art mindset into my everyday life. When I was around eleven years old, I was bullied at school. This was a year or two before I began my martial arts training. The bullying caused me to develop a depressive disorder and social anxiety. This is the reason why I began my training.

As I progressed in my martial art, I realized that the concepts used inside the dojang could apply to everyday life. Soon after beginning classes, I started to have more confidence in my abilities to take care of myself. That was instrumental in helping me to overcome what was happening to me at school.

After a year or so of training, when I had just turned fourteen, I started a relationship with a physically and mentally abusive boy at school. During this time, I had focused all my energy into making sure I did not do anything that could upset him. I was trying to avoid getting hurt. I often felt trapped, and felt as if I could not escape what was happening. My depression and anxiety became very severe, often to the point where I could not even leave my house.

By the end of the school year, my parents found out about what was happening; they removed me from school. At this point, I felt completely alone. I had no one to talk to about what happened. I became detached from life, including my martial art, although I kept attending classes.

I felt as if I had nothing in my life to look forward to, so I began to submerge myself in my martial art and soaked up all the knowledge I could. One day during class, something clicked. I do not remember exactly what changed in my mind, but I realized that I was not alone.

While it is true that Taekwon-Do is partially a physical practice, it is also a mental practice. It helped my self-confidence and reminded me that I was strong enough to make it through this turmoil. Taekwon-Do changed my entire mindset from thinking it was not my place to speak, to acknowledging that I should not allow fear to influence me anymore. The newfound confidence gave me the strength to form new friendships with the other kids; I now call them family.

Prior to my changed mindset, I was uneasy practicing self-defense or martial arts with the other men or boys in the class. I did not think someone would ever try to hurt me in real life. I eventually realized that it is a reality. I am glad that I can practice with the male martial artists in my class. It gives me even more confidence that I can make the self-defense that I learn in class work in a real-life situation.

To me, Taekwon-Do is not as much a physical art as it is mental. It builds up the fire inside that reminds me that I can do anything, and I do not have to fear anything. The people with whom I train are not just acquaintances. They are family to me. I would do anything for them. They have shown me, in return, that they would do the same for me. Thanks to my training, I am now confident in who I am.

To Thine Own Self Be True
Dana Hee

Finding myself has been my biggest wonder of self-discovery. This may have happened because I was abandoned at the age of three, or that I am the youngest child in my family. Some astrologers say it must do with the month and year in which I was born. I tend to think the wonderment of my self-discovery relates to being raised in an orphanage, where control and conformity were the name of the game.

I believe growing up in the God-fearing south, Louisiana, indoctrinated me to always be polite and never express anger or a conflicting opinion. I was taught to always be a lady, and to let the man make all the decisions. It was my job to support him in all situations. I find that it has taken more than 40 years to change my mindset and discover just who I am!

Being true to myself is the hardest lesson in my life. I have literally spent year upon year in survival mode, trying to bend the will of others, and blending into the lives of the men in my life. What I have discovered is that I am the happiest when I am just me. I am happy when I know that the life I am living includes animals, nature, peace, and harmony.

I am happy when I can pursue my career and leisure goals without reprisal or conflict with my partner. I am the happiest when I know that I am being strong and true to myself. This does not mean that I am not willing to compromise for my partner. I am very good at this because I enjoy being a giving person. I enjoy making my loved ones happy.

My discovery, that it is best to be true to myself, has been empowering. I find that I am finally able to make better choices about people in my life. I enjoy knowing that I now have boundaries and limits to what I will and will not do.

There are still times when I truly enjoy playing the role of a demure lady, yet I also revel in the excitement of risking failure to achieve my career goals. Ultimately, I find it exhilarating to live life to the fullest by just being me.

The whole secret of a successful life is to find out what is one's destiny to do, and then do it.

Henry Ford

Better Because of It
Wendy Puffenburger

Being a mother is a great gift, and I love it. After nursing both of my children, though, I was not happy with my body anymore. I decided to have a cosmetic procedure, breast augmentation surgery, to improve my looks and improve my self-confidence.

The surgery itself went well. I was recovering and starting to feel good about my body again when the unthinkable happened. Within a few months of the augmentation surgery, I received the shocking and unexpected news that I had breast cancer. There is a certain irony to attempting to improve your appearance, only to end up with the opposite, but that happened.

Prior to the actual augmentation surgery, as a concern, I asked the doctor if I needed a mammogram. She said I did not need one because breast cancer did not run in my family, and I was only thirty-three years old. I cannot stress the importance of having a mammogram, even if the doctor does not think it is necessary. If I had had the mammogram, they may have diagnosed me with Stage 1 cancer instead of Stage 2, and would have not had to have the same level of treatments.

When the doctor put the implant in my body, my immune system fought against the foreign object instead of against the growing cancer. The cancer grew at an alarmingly aggressive rate. I only had my implants for two months before I learned the devastating news.

While cancer has little to do with my interest in martial arts, it is because of my cancer that I finally decided to follow my lifelong dream of learning a martial art. I had been interested in martial arts since I was a child. I liked watching the fight scenes in the movies that showed how people defended themselves, because I went to a rough school. My parents had to work a lot and could not take me to extracurricular activities very often. Regrettably, I never had the opportunity to learn a martial art back then.

Everything in my life changed when doctors diagnosed me with cancer in 2013. I suddenly realized how short life is. I created a bucket list of all the things I always wanted to try. I quickly added learning a martial art to the list. First, I enrolled both of my kids because I wanted them to have the opportunity that I never had when I was younger.

My first class was a self-defense class with Andrea Harkins. It motivated me. I was excited to know that I still had some strength, even though I had started chemotherapy and radiation treatments and was feeling weak. My body could not do many things anymore, and it reminded me of that every day.

When I participated in the self-defense class, I said, "I can still do this!" I had an opportunity to break a board at the end of class. When I broke it, I was amazed. My mother was there and she said, "Wendy, you've still got it!" Right after that, I joined the adult martial art class and realized that was my calling. I needed to do it. Since then, cancer has derailed me from martial art practice many times, but I always return.

The type of cancer I have is triple negative breast cancer. It is not a hormonal cancer, and it is the most aggressive kind. The lump tripled in size within 3 weeks. By the date of the surgery, I had only had it for 3 months.

The initial news of the cancer came on Mother's Day. I was holding my dinner plate when the phone rang. My doctor was right to the point. I remember this as if it were yesterday. "Wendy, I have the results from your tests. It is cancerous. I'm so sorry," she said.

I fell apart at that moment. I hit the ground, crying, and my husband did not know what to do. My son was seven and cried out, "Great, my mom's going to die!" My daughter was three-years old and too young to understand.

I chose to have both of my breasts removed. I had a bilateral mastectomy on June 7, 2013. Since then, I have had several surgeries including thirty-three treatments of radiation and six months of chemotherapy.

To get through it, along with my martial art mindset, I started to go to church. One night, I dropped my daughter off for a meeting at church and felt called to go back. It was a spiritual turning point in my life. After my last treatment, I was baptized at church. Now, I am a completely different person. What was once important is no longer important to me.

My cancer journey has had many complications. After the mastectomy, there was only skin and scars left. The doctor tried to reconstruct part of one of my breasts, but the part that was radiated would not heal. She had to cut the bad tissue out and keep closing it. Each time it did not heal. Right now, I have a huge indentation where I had radiation and surgery, which is not very beautiful. Every Monday, I go to the doctor to try to expand the tissue for the reconstruction. It hurts terribly.

Am I cured? The good news is that my test results came back fine. They only schedule further tests if you complain of pain or have concerns. I am not a big complainer. I know that I still have aches, and my back bothers me, but finances prevent me from getting the tests. The doctor normally does smaller tests to rule out any new cancer.

When I finally started learning martial arts, I achieved a blue belt before I got derailed. Because my breast would not heal properly, my family insisted that I stop. Martial arts, when I am at my weakest point, make me feel strong, and that is why I always return and continue.

Now that I have been through the worst part of cancer, I feel like I can beat anything. I will keep fighting. The board break in self-defense class taught me that lesson. That was the most amazing and important milestone for me in the development of my fighting spirit and my power.

Consider just one day when you felt sick and your body was at its weakest. That is how I felt every day. When I broke the board, I felt the blood rushing through my body. It was the most amazing feeling ever because I was not that little weak girl anymore. My self-esteem jumped ten stories. It did not matter that my hair was falling out. I immediately felt like a strong and powerful woman, instead of someone who was sick.

My kids cannot wait for me to return to martial arts classes, so we can practice together again. It is only a matter of time. This time I am not going to stop. My main goal is to earn my black belt with my son. I want something we can achieve together in life. The best part about martial arts is that my children and I can learn together and create life-long memories. I look at each day and ask myself how I can make it better the next day.

Even though the black belt is my goal, it is difficult to plan for a future that you do not know. I spend a lot more time with my family now, trying to create memories. I live each day as if it could be my last. The day my son cried and thought his mama was going to die, I realized I needed to focus on creating memories for my children.

When you have a scare in your life, it changes you all the way around. This whole experience brought me closer to God and to my family. We are different in so many ways and so much closer, due to my cancer journey.

There is no telling what would happen in my life, otherwise. I am finally on the path to completing the reconstruction after struggling so long for the necessary healing to take place. I know it sounds like a very difficult journey, and it is. In some very surprising ways, it is also a blessing. Although I would never wish it on anyone else, I think I am a better person and martial artist because of it.

What seems to us as bitter trials are often blessings in disguise.
Oscar Wilde

Grateful
Rita Rose Pasquale

After four and a half years of martial art training, I became a 1st degree black belt on May 20, 1995. For some martial artists, this is the completion of their goal. For me, it was the start of my martial art journey. It is more about who you become, than the achievement of the belt. Who I was when I first started training, and who I am now, are dramatically different.

My path, at times, was very difficult and paved with discouragement. I had zero self-confidence. When I started training, I did not know anyone at my school, and there were hardly any female students. By then, due to a traumatic experience in the past, two doctors had diagnosed me with PTSD (Post Traumatic Stress Disorder).

This trauma shook me to my very core. It occurred when I was going to be an aunt for the first time, and my parents were going to be first-time grandparents. It was supposed to be a happy day for my family, and a day for which we were excited, but instead it was the opposite. My brother's first child was stillborn.

The day that should have been a celebration turned into a nightmare, instead. My brother placed the stillborn baby in my arms. It completely traumatized me. There was no way to be comforted about this loss. Most people did not know what to say. I heard some of the most insensitive remarks, which only made the pain worse.

After the PTSD diagnosis, I decided to do two things to get well again. I went to counseling, and I joined a martial arts school. I knew that if I did not do something, my anxiety would spin out of control.

I began my training in September 1991. One month after I started classes, my father had a nervous breakdown and was hospitalized. I remember telling my instructor that I was not coming to class for a while. I was shocked when he screamed at me, "How can you take care of your family, when you aren't taking care of yourself?"

I was so angry. I thought the nerve of this man to speak to me like this, with all I have going on in my life. Looking back now, I thank God for what he said. He was right, and it was a revelation for me.

During my training, I met my husband, Anthony, and we dated for three years before getting married. We have been married for more than twenty years. In June, our studio will be twenty-one years old. He has gone through thick and thin with me. With PTSD, I could not drive on the highway. My husband had to take me for a dry run if I had to drive.

I was so fearful that I could not even go through a car wash or on an amusement park ride. Whenever we went to an event, like a concert, or to the ballet, I was uncomfortable. This was embarrassing and a huge inconvenience for me. I never knew when a panic attack was going to hit. If it happened during a class, or even worse, during a test, I felt like I was having a heart attack.

The good news is I am no longer that woman. I do not often talk about these topics anymore, but I want people to see how far I have really come, thanks to martial arts. If I can do it, anyone can. Whatever your fear, you must face it, or it will get bigger.

If you have anxiety, there is hope, but you must be willing to do the work. In my twenty-five years of martial arts training, I have also studied and practiced yoga, and meditation. I once thought that martial arts and yoga were the same. There are similarities, but they are very different. Martial arts are about movement, and yoga is about stillness. Meditation is an amazing way to quiet the mind and connect with your breath.

In the last three years, I have been working with a life coach and lifeline practitioner, Dean Schafer, who has helped me learn new ways to cope with fear, anxiety, and stress. I have learned how to catch myself being fearful or negative. It is a learned skill, just like martial arts.

One of the greatest lessons he has shared is, "Fear is the result of mentally living in the future, so do your best to stay in the now." I use this philosophy to teach children about anxiety, and when I see that they understand, it is a great gift to me.

When I was younger, I felt like I was different and I hated having anxiety. I now look at it as a gift because I know exactly how others feel when they have fear and cannot participate in a class. I love teaching, and I love helping people.

By sharing my story, I hope that it will inspire others to realize that if I can overcome, they can, too. I know that if I didn't go through this trauma and rebuilding of my life, I would not have learned life lessons or be where I am today – a 3rd degree black belt, Sifu, and studio owner working with children, some with anxiety.

Through all of this, I thoroughly enjoy teaching children to have empathy, and to be charitable in their own communities. At my studio, we sponsor several fundraising events for charities and our community. To date, with the help of my students, we have raised more than $70,000.00 for St. Jude Children's Research Hospital.

This fundraising inspired me to start a cookie business, "Sifu Rita's Kitchen," where I bake and sell cookies to raise money for St. Jude. I also film a cooking show once a month on the local community television channel.

I still feel fear, but the difference is that I no longer allow it to hold me back. Martial arts training and my faith in God have become the anchors in my life. They keep my feet on the ground. I am grateful for everything I have learned, and especially that I can teach and help my students find their own path.

A Real Martial Artist
Andrea Harkins

Someone once criticized me and said that I am not a real martial artist. I know that there are fakes out there and those who only teach to make money, but I am not one of them. A fake might try to trick you with false credentials, or a false rank, or degree. I put in many years of hard work, and even though my traditional practice contained a few less-than-traditional parts, I am still a real martial artist.

Still, it made me examine the question. Could it be true? Am I not a real martial artist? The real martial artists have a mission and a purpose. They learn and subsequently teach what they know, support their students, and promote a positive mindset. That seems to describe me accurately.

When I became more involved in a broader group of martial artists around the world through social media, I noticed that the same issues permeate everywhere. No matter where you are, there are fakes, but they have never been worthy of my very valuable time or energy.

You cannot control what others think or say about you. You must create a solid background, be truthful about what you know and who you are, and see how it shakes out. There will always be haters. The important thing is to focus on bettering yourself and to simply disregard criticism and negativity.

I am not traditional or trendy; I fall somewhere in between. I have held 2nd degree black belt since 1997. I intermingle martial art words from different languages, which freaks out traditional practitioners. Others have accused me of learning everything wrong.

If I could make a new category of martial artist, it would be for someone like me, a woman whose styles are still blended but still important and relevant. That should exempt me from having to try to be something I am not, or from having to live up to others' false expectations that I am not real.

Being a real martial artist is about applying martial arts to daily life. That attribute is what makes the difference. As far as perfection is concerned, I have yet to see the martial artist who understands, comprehends, and applies every martial art nuance to their art. We all have some work to do in this never-ending journey. Maybe none of us is real.

I am not a martial art superstar and will never claim to be. I have some decent skills and I am working on learning a new style. I am what I consider an everyday martial artist, and there are a lot of us out there. I teach, learn, encourage, and care, day to day, week to week, and year to year. I have never let my martial art practice or mindset wander far. Four children, varying careers, difficulties, and getting older have all consistently required that I keep my martial art mindset. That is a long time to be consistent or dedicated to anything.

I have changed and evolved during this long-time span in martial arts. At some point, the real martial artist in me started to focus on helping others. In the beginning, a martial art practice is like infancy, with a focus on self. Later, it becomes a time of exploration and growth, then maturity, and that is where I am today.

As a woman in the martial arts, I have discovered that this shifting of focus away from yourself to others is what makes martial arts real. They become an example by which to live life, and an essential method of communication. If you continue to train and learn, then you must make room to motivate and inspire others along the way.

If you want to apply a martial art mindset or spirit to your life, or you want to make martial arts real, examine your difficulties and obstacles. How can you overcome these? What is your reaction time? Utilizing a martial art mindset and positive approach, you will recover more quickly from even the most difficult situations. It does not take the obstacle away, but helps you to work through it more efficiently, in an ambitious and steadfast way.

Are you living the life you want, or are you getting through each day without any positive flow of energy? Understand your strengths and push through your barriers using a positive force. Break through the obstacles that stop you from being the real person you want to be.

For the person who criticized me for not being real, I ask, does consistent practice and teaching for twenty-seven years make me real? What does it mean that I almost adopted two of my own students when their caregiver unexpectedly passed away? Does constant outreach, teaching free, or motivating others through martial arts, credit me with being real? I think I have enough ammunition to buffer the criticism about being real.

My goal here has little to do with highlighting myself as a martial artist. In fact, my mission and calling is about spreading good messages and life lessons through martial arts. I heard a calling one day that spoke these words to me, "If you want to be a real martial artist, make a real difference."

Martial Art Lessons
Restita DeJesus

I was a martial art child. It took me many years to grow into a martial art woman, and finally understand who she is. She is comfortable in her own skin and presses on regardless of obstacles in her way. She asks for help when she needs it, and never wants anyone, especially men, to think of her as a helpless waif. With confidence and compassion, she has an edge that can be honed or dulled, depending on the circumstance.

I started martial arts in 1978, for three reasons. First, my great grandfather, Santiago Toledo, was a well-known Filipino Martial arts master, and I wanted to learn his legendary practice. Secondly, as a premature baby, born at 24 weeks, I was told that I had a fighting spirit, and I wanted to apply that to my life. Thirdly, I wanted to be like Kwai Chang Caine from the old *Kung Fu* TV series.

My parents enrolled my sister and me in karate. While it was not the same as *Kung Fu* on television, I liked it. I became obsessed with everything martial arts related, including books, television shows, and magazines. I practiced every day, and took to heart the philosophy of "no fighting unless absolutely necessary." Even as a child, I had fantasies of being an all-knowing master.

I was one of only a few girls in the kids' martial arts class, and later, one of a very few women in adult class. Fortunately, I did not experience discrimination, but I did experience a few situations that made me rethink my passion for the martial arts.

It was ironic that as soon as I began martial arts lessons as a child, bullies found me. I never told anyone that I practiced karate. A neighbor boy followed me to school every day, kicking my lunchbox, pushing me, and calling me awful names. I knew I could kick him, but my martial art did not allow it. I stood my ground, yet did not defend myself verbally or be drawn into fruitless physical aggression. That is when I learned important lessons about martial arts and dealing with bullies.

Lesson 1: Martial arts teach confidence. I was afraid to demand that the bully stop. I did not tell him to stop, so his bullying behavior continued every morning. One day, I finally had enough. I was having a grumpy morning, my umbrella turned inside out, and my shoes were soaked from the Seattle rain.

Bully boy kicked my lunchbox one too many times, and I turned right around, raised my pointy umbrella in a two handed bo grip, and screamed at the top of my lungs "Stop it or I'll put this right down your throat!" This led me to lesson two.

Lesson 2: Never use Karate in anger. Did I find my confidence? Yes, but I found it when I was engulfed in crazy, strong anger. Bully Boy yelled, "You ain't got no Kung Fu, you're just a dumb girl," and I let loose with a swing that landed the umbrella to the side of his head. He fell down crying and I yelled out in anger, "How does it feel to cry, Dumbo?" and I stomped away. Inside I cringed because hitting in anger was a no-no, and I blatantly broke that rule.

Lesson 3: Learn fighting etiquette from your martial art practice. Never revel in the defeat of your kumite partner was the rule. Help your partner improve, and you will improve. Celebrating another's defeat teaches you nothing. I completely forgot that lesson in my moment of anger. I remember feeling justified, powerful, and willful.

I hit him, and broke the cardinal rule about hitting unless necessary. I ran home and told my parents what happened. My father went to speak with the neighbor boy's parents, and later that day we heard the boy's screams all the way around the block, as he received a spanking. The next morning, I heard running feet behind me. Thinking it was the bully, I wheeled around with my hands up in fighting posture.

Surprisingly, he apologized and so did I. He visited my karate class and even tried a few lessons before he and his family moved away. That experience stuck with me through my teen years. I learned that it was okay to be angry, but not okay to strike out in anger. It paved the way for how I approached training through my turbulent teenage phase.

Through these life lessons, I had a supportive karate teacher and classmates. There was no sexism or differences in the way boys and girls received training. Equality was a driving force. I received my black belt in 1982 at the age of 15, and that is when my motivation for self-improvement went into overdrive.

I decided to learn other martial arts to supplement my training. As I began, I started to question if I looked too much like a tomboy. I finally realized that martial training does not compromise femininity. I am sure some women have found themselves acting like "one of the guys" to get through class. I know I did. I was lucky enough to train with boys and men who accepted me and the other feminine students without prejudice. It was not until later in my life when I felt the need to prove myself.

At some seminars, I had a lower ranking male student as a partner, who had no idea that I outranked him. He refused to punch at my head in self-defense drills. "Punch at my head," I said, to which he responded, "Well, we'll go slowly because I don't want to hurt you."

Actions like these do not help a woman learn to protect herself. I said to him, "I thought you were here as my training partner, to help me learn how to react in dangerous situations. If I get hit, I learn a great lesson." Then, I promptly raised my hand and requested a new training partner.

At another time, in a different style that I was learning, smirks and remarks such as, "I don't want to hurt you," would surface. It made me seethe inside because my partners were beginners, just like me. Although I already held a black belt, they did not know it, and it seemed that they assumed I was a weak Asian girl. When I executed a technique, and dropped them to the floor, they complained that I had a chip on my shoulder or could not control myself.

Did I have a chip on my shoulder? In a way, I did. I wanted to prove that I could do exactly what they could do. My overuse of power did not help my case much, though. I had to tone it down so others would not think of me as the crazy girl with the attitude.

In yet another class, some of the men who were lower-ranked than I was, made blatant sexual innuendos and lewd remarks about my black belt status. By this point in my training, I had learned how to stand my ground. I calmly asserted, "My skill and my rank should garner respect, simply because of my skill and rank. My ass has nothing to do with my skill. Do I make myself clear?"

Lesson 4: Stand up for what you believe is right and just. As the years passed, I found that standing up for what I believed, as well as doing my best as a student and a teacher, helped me improve my life, regardless of petty misogynistic comments or poor behavior by men. I passed many of these lessons on to my own students.

One lesson that I learned was the result of a life test. In 2001, I sustained a spine injury that resulted in chronic peripheral neuropathy. The endless painful pins and needles feelings, frequent total numbness in my feet and hands, and back pain, resulted in more than two years of tearful recovery. I often incorrectly landed on my feet because I could not feel them, or dropped things because I could not feel my hands. I had to train myself to walk correctly again.

Privately I struggled and cried about it. Martial arts were my life. There was no way I could see myself quitting because of my injury. I grew worried when my neurologist was unable to pinpoint how long the recovery would be, or even if I would ever regain normal function.

I took tests for spinal tumors, multiple sclerosis, diabetes, and other illnesses, all of which were inconclusive. My neurologist hinted that I should start making life changes. The maxim, "Hard in training, easy in battle," immediately came to my mind.

I had been through physical trials in my martial arts training before and wanted to quit. I had pain that was unbearable, broken bones, a bloody face, and dislocated joints. The battle of recovery through this spinal injury would be no different. I had to remember to keep an attitude of going forward, and never backwards.

Tai Chi helped me focus on my body movement and become aware of every thought and every move. The concept of "correction through the flow," made a profound impact on my recovery. Today, I have recovered, mostly. On occasion, if I sit incorrectly, my feet and hands send me a tingly reminder to correct my posture and attitude. In many ways, attitude is your posture.

Lesson 5: Become like a needle wrapped in cotton. This lesson is about having a strong, unbendable core, sheathed with a flexible shell. Personally, I have withstood many storms, but finally achieved my childhood dream of being a martial art woman ranked as a master. I must continually practice to get better.

Continually practice what you are good at, too. Celebrate each step of "Do, the way" because once you take each step, you master the process of getting there. This progression is what creates a strong and confident martial arts woman.

Every new day offers a new learning experience. There are no predictions and no criteria. I have learned an abundance of lessons from my very public application to martial arts. It has also been a very personal and private endeavor. Each of these lessons is just as applicable to life, as they are to martial arts.

Krav Maga Changed My Life
Kelina Cowell

I started Krav Maga in 2008 while living in Leicester, UK. I had been on a break from martial arts after quitting Muay Thai eight years earlier due to a serious knee injury I sustained from a kick. I had to learn how to walk again.

After eighteen months of physiotherapy, my doctors told me that martial arts training was no longer an option for me. I believed them and became very depressed. I also became morbidly obese and weighed in at 308lbs. I was suffering from high blood pressure and a spinal condition called Hyper-Lordosis. As the only one in my family without diabetes, I was fearful that it, too, would raise its ugly head in a matter of time.

On January 1, 2008, I looked at myself in the mirror and decided I could not live like that anymore. I needed to get my life back. I felt like I was not living, but simply existing, and there is a huge difference between the two.

I gradually began training at home, because I was too shy to go to the gym. I lost 14 pounds in my first month of home training and healthy eating. I then had the confidence to start looking for a martial art that would work around my knee injury and spinal condition.

I knew there was something out there for me after seeing so many disabled people training in martial arts. I discovered Krav Maga, and I wanted to see what it was. In no time, I was hooked and never looked back.

After surviving several violent and abusive events in my life and training in different martial arts, Krav Maga was the style that finally conquered my demons. It installed enough confidence in myself that I knew I would never be a victim again. It set me free from years of abuse that had infiltrated my life, starting when I was just 5 or 6 years old.

On my first day in a girl's youth group back then, the woman in charge of the group locked me in a cupboard (closet) until it was time to go home. I cannot remember what I did wrong. I didn't tell my parents because I thought I would get into more trouble for being naughty, and I had no idea that being locked in a cupboard was wrong. After that, I refused to join other clubs, or I quit after a couple of sessions. I did not know how to socialize with other kids, and adults scared me.

A close family friend around the age of nine also sexually abused me, until I hit puberty. Because of this, I was very withdrawn throughout my childhood.

At the age of 11, I typically went swimming by myself early before school. I was bullied a lot at school and swimming was my personal time to calm my anxiety and focus on myself. The swimming pool was unstaffed at that time, and this morning there was an old man in the pool. He called out to me saying he had a cramp in his leg and asked me to help him.

When we got to the ladder, he pinned me against it and stuck his hand inside my swimming suit between my legs. I kicked him off and managed to swim to another ladder, and leave.

I reported it to a lifeguard, who was sitting in a nearby room eating his breakfast. He seemed quite annoyed that I was interrupting, and he had no interest in finding the man who was still somewhere in the building. Nothing happened about it. I never went back. I quit swimming all together. I did not even tell my parents about it until years later.

I was also verbally bullied at school, for being of mixed race. My father is white, of British descent, and my mother is Maltese, of North African descent. When I was 15, I had an argument with a friend and she took revenge by telling other kids in our class a personal secret of mine. The secret managed to circulate around all 2,000 students in the entire school within a day. After that, they physically bullied me, too.

During an awards ceremony, a girl ran up behind me on stage and pulled my skirt up in front of the entire school. I was regularly spat on, to the point that I would hide in the bathroom until the bell rang causing me to arrive late to every class. I was also followed home daily and had stones and dog feces thrown at me. The lowest point was when someone poured a bottle of urine over my head.

I reported every incident to my teachers, but nothing happened about it. I started retaliating by getting into fights in my final year of high school, and often ditching school.

I have also been in two knife attacks. The first was when I was 16. I was out clubbing with a friend and she decided to leave. I decided to take a taxi home. At 3:00 a.m. I stood alone on a quiet street waiting for a taxi.

This was my main mistake because I was too lazy to walk to the taxi rank. At that age, with a lack of personal safety awareness, and clouded by my anger towards my friend, I chose to wait near the club where taxis usually drove past. This evening, however, it was deserted.

Within minutes, a group of older teens found me and took the opportunity to terrorize me. They shoved me against the wall, and put a knife to my neck, all because of my goth fashion and the purple streaks in my hair.

At the time, I had Muay Thai training, which is what helped me persevere through all the high school bullying. I always reacted with a fight response. I had the skills to deal with fists, kicks, and hair pulling in school, but this was bullying on a new level. I was drunk, and they pinned me up against a wall in the middle of the night, with a knife to my throat. I did not know how to defend against that.

All I remember is this girl shouting, "You think you're better than us, not so cool now are ya?" into my face, and her friends shouting, "Cut her, cut her!" I reduced to a mumbling, stuttering wreck, which they found highly amusing. Lucky for me, a passer-by stopped and diffused the situation.

I do not know if he said something or if they were bored of the game they were playing, but the bully let go of me and joined the rest in conversation. I managed to stumble away and get into a nearby taxi. It was from that point that I decided I needed to look at self-defense training beyond striking skills.

The second knife attack was over a year ago. A junkie approached me outside my flat late at night, in Stockwell, South London. He lunged at my stomach with a box cutter. My training kicked in, and I handled it as if it was a drill in class. I had no hesitation, fear, or questions, and immediately reacted. I do not remember thinking anything, but I do remember watching his hands and reacting instinctively when he pulled out something shiny.

It was not until I got inside and slammed the door behind me that I noticed my heart was pounding outside my chest, and my body was shaking with adrenaline. This was a vastly difference response compared to 17 years ago, and I owe that to my Krav Maga training.

I have been in two abusive relationships, the first when I was fifteen and dating a seventeen-year-old, who would burn me with cigarettes for any minor reason. The second was in my early to mid-twenties, and was mostly mental abuse because of my weight. I became a recluse and did not want to leave our apartment. My anxiety problems increased, and I started having panic attacks often.

The abuse by my partner became physical towards the end of the relationship. I had lost all the weight by then and was teaching Krav Maga. One day, I finally had enough. Instead of simply releasing the choke and trying to get away, I released and hit back.

The courage to strike someone you love is not as easy as defending against a stranger on the street. You need to experience domestic violence to understand that. It extends far beyond physical abuse, and is not as black and white as you may think. There are mind games, apologies, and promises that cloud your judgement.

On the day after I struck back, I was never bothered about it again. I relocated to London shortly after to start a new chapter in my life. I had reached a boiling point in my life and enough was enough.

This was finally when I had evolved enough mentally to realize that I was strong, that I deserved better, and that I was not going to tolerate it any more. People will be shocked when they read these stories about me, especially because I am such a different person today. They may not expect these stories, but now they know. Krav Maga changed my life, and maybe even saved it.

The starting point of all achievement is desire.

Napoleon Hill

Ageless
Andrea Harkins

When I joined martial arts as a young woman, I did not realize all the health benefits that I would experience from my practice, until I began to evolve into a middle-aged practitioner. In a sense, each martial art workout was like putting another credit into my life meter.

Flexibility, bone strength, muscularity, stamina, and joint movement are some of the benefits that have allowed me to maintain a youthful life. Even now in my 50's I attribute my overall health and youthful demeanor wholly to my martial arts training and the cultivation of a strong mindset.

I am as agile as a much younger person is. I do not need to take any necessary medications. In fact, the doctor calls me his "star patient," and reads my lab work like it is poetry. He is thrilled to see someone my age who is not struggling with a myriad of issues. I have no concerns as compared to many other women my age.

I do not wake up in pain every morning. In fact, I feel little or no aches or pains whatsoever. When I stretch, I continue to maintain or even achieve increased flexibility. I participate in any workouts that I want. I have no physical limitations. I have enough energy to accomplish what I need to finish. I have a good, balanced, positive way of thinking.

I am no doctor, but the fact is that unlike some other 50-something year old women, I do not struggle with weight issues, or mood swings. Because my martial art mindset is always in constant motion, I still feel youthful inside and out, and others have told me that I look that way, too.

It is very true that there are different exercises and sports that will keep you in shape, but none have the dual benefits of mindset and physicality that martial arts have. They are the closest thing that I have found to a makeshift, philosophical fountain of youth. The fountain continually spews strength of body, mind, and spirit.

Martial arts help me feel secure, vibrant, and youthful. I have gone to class dead tired, or even with sore muscles from another workout, only to completely forget those issues during class. The stretching and performance of the martial art skills revive and refresh me.

Still, not everyone agrees that martial arts are a great choice, but they do not know what I have experienced through my practice. Being a student of a martial art, whether trendy, ancient, or traditional, has a lot to offer to the everyday woman. There may be occasional injuries along the way or hard challenges, but overall, it promotes wellness, health, and personal achievement.

My friend, Patricia Roth, practices Taekwondo. She is a 2nd degree black belt working toward her 3rd degree, and she describes her journey as the best, healthiest, and happiest time of her life. She is a student and an instructor. She loves her martial art life and plans to be involved as long as possible.

Like me, Pat has used her martial art training and mindset to cope with some extremely difficult times. She regained her confidence and sense of self through her martial art. She tells other women, "Make your passion a part of your life and you won't regret it! The only regret is if you never try."

Pat does not expect to be the best martial artist in the world, but she sets high expectations to meet her own personal short and long-term goals. None of this information is mind-blowing, except for the fact that Pat is fifty-nine years young, and just started her martial arts journey a few years ago.

No matter who you are, how old you are, or what obstacles stand in your way, following a lifelong passion will make you a better and more youthful you. Pat and I found commonality in our age and gender, martial art training, and teaching. In my opinion, she and I are aging in the very best way, by applying a martial art mindset to our everyday lives. She has learned to be more focused and well-rounded now, than any other time in her life. It is as if she reversed the hands of time.

The best defense against aging is keeping active and purposeful. When I see women just starting their martial art journey in their 50's, 60's, or 70's, I am personally renewed. When any woman combines the different aspects of a martial art into her life, she becomes more than a woman who practices a martial art. She experiences a renewed self.

The Award-Winning Vision of Jennifer Linch
Andrea Harkins

Jennifer Linch used her martial art practice and experiences to secure a foothold in the movie industry. Her film, *The Dream*, won the Best Newcomer award at the World Film Awards in June 2015, and Honorable Mention at La Neo Noir Film Festival. Her movie, *Flowers of The Night*, won the Grand Prize at ICannes International Film Festival in July 2015. In August 2015, she received awards for Best Action Picture and Best Actress at the La Neo Noir Film Festival.

As if those were not enough, her accomplishments also include an International Silver Award for directing and an International Silver Award for Screenplay and Story from the International Film Competition. She was nominated for Best Film, Best Brutal Fight Scene, and Best Female Director for Fight Sequence at the Urban Action Film Festival, and Most Favorite Film, at International Film Competition.

This talented actor and director would have never found success in the movie industry, if not for her journey as a female martial artist. Her pursuit and passion for martial arts began when she was twelve years old. As a young girl, she frequently got ill. Her brother, a martial art master, believed that martial arts could make her stronger and healthier, so he made her study them. It worked! She's been practicing ever since.

As Jennifer progressed in her training, to maintain her health, she began to apply patience and discipline to her martial arts, as well as to her life. She began to feel even stronger, both physically and mentally. As a girl trained in the martial arts, she no longer "yells like a girl" and feels that if she is hit, she is strong enough to take the force. This paves the way for her martial art movie creativity.

Mentally, Jennifer uses the martial art discipline to control her inner demons. Through her own martial art practice, she can control anger and be humble, especially during the long hours she spends on a film set. She would not be a martial art movie director, if she did not have years of martial arts training that give her an inside edge to writing, directing, and casting appropriate actors for her movies.

As an action star, Jennifer strives to practice martial arts four to five times a week, and she eats vegan foods. She never reveals her age, but she exudes transcendent youthfulness.

Jennifer Linch has taken a martial art path that few other martial art women get to travel, as a movie actor and director. She continues to excel by using martial arts to excite and entertain audiences, through her award-winning martial art vision.

All our dreams can come true if we have the courage to pursue them.

Walt Disney

Femininity

The only person you are destined to become is the person you decide to be.

Ralph Waldo Emerson

Uncompromised Femininity
Andrea Harkins

If you had to describe me, one word that you might use is feminine. I wear a skirt or a dress and heels nearly every day, and I have wavy hair that flows down the center of my back. I enjoy fashion, make-up and many things that enhance who I am as a woman.

Most people think of a martial arts woman as someone who is athletic, physically strong, or has a very dominant personality. What they forget is that martial arts suit every personality, including the feminine, the masculine, the young, or the old. My gender and my age really have no bearing on whether I can learn a martial art.

Martial arts do not change a woman's demeanor or her personality. If she is a feminine woman, she remains that. Just because there is an aggressive aspect to her training that may appear masculine or powerful, it does not diminish anything else about her.

The most feminine woman can learn a martial art. The fighting and escape techniques, katas, and other skills that are required, do not demand a change in personality, just one in the thought process.

Training does not consider what a female student looks like, what kind of clothes she wears, or if she is feminine or not. There are no masculine attributes to kicks, punches, or yells. The mindfulness, balance, and centeredness that martial arts offer is the same for men and women, neither masculine nor feminine. The only difference is that women can bring femininity to power. They will experience enhanced confidence, through which they will become stronger, more powerful women.

Never once did I compromise my true self, or my beliefs, in my martial arts practice. There are a few insights I learned that I did not realize prior to my training. One insight was that when compared to a man, I could just as easily break a hold, take a fall, manipulate, train, and increase my personal power. My only inhibitions are in my own mind, and nothing else, not gender or femininity.

Those who do not believe that my techniques will really work because I am a feminine woman often challenge me. The disbelief about if I can disengage from a hold usually comes in a joke form, but I know that behind the joke, the question is a serious one.

My sparring partners are curious as to how I can protect, defend, or escape, because it is an unexpected behavior. In my everyday life, I seem less a fighter than I do when I am barefoot on the dojo floor in my uniform.

Shy of asking my friends to grab me so I can show what I know, I usually deflect the conversation, as I would try to de-escalate any unwanted situation.

It is not that I do not want to show what I can do. I would just rather not share my defensive techniques and strategies outside the dojo.

I think women are less likely to be drawn into the trap of "showing what they know," than men. I have no problem with others questioning my abilities. I will allow them to conjecture that I cannot defend myself. It really does not matter to me. There is no need to show off just because my ego gets a little hurt.

Some think that a feminine woman is always appreciative, helpful, sincere, caring, and kind. I cannot dispute that she may have some of these attributes. Learning a martial art might be the very first time in her life when she learns self-defense concepts. Her martial art practice gives her the opportunity to punch, push, shove, and fight aggressively. To think of her tightened fist striking flesh and bone is startling. It I not what she has been trained to do as a woman.

There will always be differences between male and female martial artists, even if they train the same. However, the feminine woman is just as capable of learning a martial art as a man. My advice to all female martial artists is just remain true to who you are.

What I learned from practicing a martial art is that I will never give in, or give up, without a fight. Does that in any way compromise my femininity? Not in my book!

What is Femininity in Martial Arts?
Jackie Bradbury

I do not know what femininity means, to be honest. It runs the gamut in popular culture from Shirley Temple, to Barbie, to Xena Warrior Princess, and everything in between. From a stereotypical point of view, it may mean being passive, or a woman who values relationships over achievements. Some may define it as being nurturing, graceful, overly emotional, dependent, prized for looks and sex appeal, lacking logic or intelligence, or being frivolous and weak.

These character traits have never been my view of femininity. I was not raised that way, nor was my mother, and I am not raising my two daughters that way either. If martial arts training is compromising this stereotypical idea of femininity, I say, "Good!" The idea of the helpless, weak female concerned with frivolous things and needing protection by men needs to be changed.

There is plenty of room for what we have come to think of as female traits in martial arts. The feminine side has a place in some arts, like aikido, where passivity is in context. Below you will find other examples of female traits that are useful in martial arts.

Intuition. A woman's intuition is how she gathers non-verbal cues from the people around her. Men, on the other hand, do not recognize non-verbal communication in the same way. They do not use intuition to avoid violent conflicts in the same way women do.

Trainability. Some say that women are more trainable than men are, because they come to training with few preconceived notions and have an open mind to the teaching. That is an attitude with which men seem to struggle.

Practice. Because women rarely have the reach, height, weight, or strength advantage, they must work hard to perfect technique and concepts. They cannot depend on a physical or strength advantage to sustain them.

The problem with strength is that it will eventually dissipate during aging. If you learn proper technique initially, you will not lose as much ability that you would if you rely solely on strength or physical power. For proof of this, look at old masters of the martial arts. They are just as deadly as ever, even if they are weaker than when they were younger.

I think of my training experience as something beyond gender or sex. I am short, middle aged, of a normal fitness level, and have average upper body strength. This could describe anybody, male or female. At the same time, I cannot ignore the reality of what being female means for me, especially in a male dominated environment.

Many people, male and female, will never believe that I can hold my own in a violent confrontation. Some people will think that what I do is unbecoming and unladylike. There still exist some problems in the martial arts world today with sexual bias and harassment.

None of this, however, defines what kind of woman I am. I earn respect by being good at what I do. If others think that makes me less of a woman, that is their problem, not mine.

Blood and Oxygen
Michelle Manu

Femininity can never be lost, but it can be unknown or underdeveloped. Femininity is as sure as the blood and oxygen that flows through our veins. In the Hawaiian culture, the fire goddess, Pele, is attributed the birth and life of the Hawaiian people. She is still very revered by the people as the Goddess, not just the Goddess of Fire. Wisdom is the core of femininity.

In ancient times, when missionaries or warriors from different islands or tribes appeared, some kahunas say the women warriors met those trespassers. They were ready to defend their territory and loved ones. They credit the women with interceding with the Divine and the birth of all living things.

Women protected the villages, including the land, people, and offspring, when the men were off to battle. Still to this day, it is women who diligently and honorably govern as chiefs and leaders in many South Pacific, Native American, and Aboriginal nations.

Women have discredited the divinity of the feminine and their nature on many levels. They need continual strengthening of their instincts to schedule time for themselves to nurture their desires. They also need to know when to nurture and rejuvenate or let go, to care of others in a non-codependent way. Personally, this has been a difficult process for me. It is difficult for me to schedule and keep time to myself.

"They [women] are not to see, and instead to "make pretty," all manner of grotesqueries whether they are lovely or not. This early training to be nice causes women to override their intuitions…" Clarissa Pinkola Estes, Ph.D., *Women Who Run with the Wolves.*

We live in a society where, up until recently, only our masculine traits were worthy of strength, endurance, honor, and heroism. There is no gender in the spirit, so it is my opinion that women should no longer quench, suppress, or condemn their desires to endure, thrive, be an everyday hero, or be a healthy female.

An everyday hero is someone, regardless of gender, who evaluates what would be the best decision for all involved, and does what needs to be finished, no matter how difficult, and does not whine about it.

Our society often classifies women in two ways: whore or saint. I dislike labels and choose to think that women are either a healthy, or unhealthy, feminine. A healthy feminine is a woman who acknowledges and understands her areas of development, while unapologetically maintaining her power and gracefully using her strengths.

A healthy female chooses wisely to express herself, not from a place of having to prove herself, but because she does not have to prove herself. She has a quiet, resonating, and uncompromising spiritual strength that others feel when in her presence.

An unhealthy feminine is a woman who does not evaluate herself or her life. Her primary focus is on the external and on appearances. Because of her intended appearance of perfection, she speaks in an unloving, self-critical, and judgmental tone. This causes her to fall further into a vortex where she tries to reach externally for her worth.

This is also the woman who defaults to sleeping with her martial arts instructors, posts less than respectful photos and comments on social media, and has no problem verbally attacking another woman with the same self-critical standards she holds for herself. It is a type of woman-on-woman bullying which is not always recognized. This behavior is life depleting, not life giving.

If any woman must compromise who she is at her core, or discredit her intent, then her current environment is not the correct one for her enlightenment, advancement, and self-discovery. She already knows this, but is often not courageous enough to make the right decisions for herself.

If she does not learn the lesson the first time, similar events will present themselves repeatedly. Through her practice, a woman's awareness and choice of remaining a healthy female always remains within her; femininity can never be lost.

Half Clad
Andrea Harkins

I am not lucky to be a female martial artist. I did not pick a four-leaf clover or perform a magic spell to join the rank of female martial artists in this world. I put in all the work and effort just like any man, and I withstood the test of time.

Luck has nothing to do with earning a black belt. It did not give me the ability to teach others the physically and mentally demanding application of martial arts. There is only one way that luck came into this at all. I was lucky enough to believe in myself.

I admit that I was out of shape and a little lazy in the beginning. Thankfully, I slowly transformed into the woman I am today, a practitioner of traditional martial arts. I love so many things about martial arts, including the focus, self-discipline, and sense of personal accomplishment.

I see the traditional martial arts woman as a smart and adept individual, strong, and persuasive, but I do not necessarily see her the way the media portrays her. If you hinged your beliefs on the marketing of the martial art woman, you might believe that all female martial artists are beautiful, immaculately fit, and wear a skimpy bra top, small boy shorts, and a pretty pair of fighting gloves when they practice. The portrayal of the traditional martial arts woman in these ads does not remind me of me.

I saw a blog post recently about the best reasons to practice a traditional martial art. This is a great topic and something every aspiring martial artist should read, but the accompanying photograph made me think twice. It was a woman wearing exactly what I just described.

I could not connect in my own mind how she practiced a traditional martial art wearing that. Just comfort wise, it does not work. I have yet to work out with a female martial artist who wore such little clothing or whose stomach was flatter than the boards we break in class.

I realize it is marketing or a way to catch the eye of a purchaser. This woman is a model, and her job is to look good to sell products. All advertising uses sex appeal on some level. I am not naïve, and I am not trying to make anyone believe that this kind of marketing is not effective. It works.

My main pet peeve about this is deeper than just some small argument that I am not nearly as beautiful or fit as the martial art model. My concern is that it will dissuade woman and girls from ever trying a martial art, even if they are interested.

Girls, especially, already have so many pressures to look a certain way. The dojo should be one of the few places where they can blend in without worrying about their body image. It is a place where they should excel based on their personal practice, dedication, and commitment, and not how their body is shaped or how beautiful their face is.

When did beauty enter the picture? The female martial artist has the same ambitions as any martial artist, to increase her power, focus, drive, ambition, and act. She is not participating so she can walk a runway in a beauty pageant. It is the age-old "sex sells" mentality, and it is not something that is going to go away anytime soon.

Will the media perception of a traditional female practitioner convince girls or women not to attend a class when they already struggle with insecurities? Will they ignore the opportunity because they do not look like the martial art model on the poster?

I suppose the crux of this is that I see a martial art as something more than a product or a service. It is a time-honored tradition that deserves respect. Female martial artists are finally making headway, becoming mainstream, and being accepted and respected martial artists. Will the portrayal of a half-naked female martial artist in the media negate this long-desired respect factor?

I have nothing to prove here, other than just bringing up a topic that many overlook. I want nothing to stand in the way of any girl or woman trying a martial art, no matter her age, shape, or physical condition. Her motivation should come from within and not be a desire to improve herself because she thinks others want her to look or act a certain way. She must see herself as someone who can learn and achieve through a martial arts practice, no matter how she looks.

I admit, being a female black belt creates the aura that a woman is strong and powerful woman. I do not want the world to compare or mistake the hard-working, efficient, traditional female martial artist with some half-clad model. I do not want girls or women to avoid learning a martial art because they feel like they do not measure up or fit the mold.

As a female martial artist, I know that I have made great strides in my life, and it is not luck that I got this far. I hope the same happens for any girl or woman who has an interest in learning a martial art.

This all begs the question, what does the traditional female martial artist look like to you? No matter what a woman wears in her practice, traditional, or not, I hope that you see her for who she is. Luckily, in either example, she is a lot more on the inside because of her martial arts training.

The Power Degree
Andrea Harkins

The martial arts woman has power! If you do not know her, you might question her strength and fortitude, but trust me, she has what everyone on this planet wants, a powerhouse in life. She has control of life's steering wheel and can maneuver in any direction she wants. The choice is hers, and she will forever use it to her benefit.

It is easy to see the power of martial artists. With a kick, a punch, or a turn, a practitioner has what it takes to thrive. The key to that kind of power is practice, resilience, and patience. A woman must learn these skills. They are not innate. Through this learning and recognition of ability, she earns her power degree.

Physical power is easy to define. The female martial artist will see improvement in her body over time. She may work hard enough to gain muscle mass, lose weight, or decrease body fat. When she gets stronger, she is glad that she applied herself, even when she was tired, sore, or lacked inspiration. She is flexing and strengthening both physical and mental muscles.

Who deserves the powerful woman label? I will happily step forward. As a female martial artist, and black belt, I am part of a small percentage of women who practice and teach. Then, I am part of another smaller group of women who have been dedicated to martial arts for more than 25 years, part of even a smaller group who teach a family owned martial art program, and an even smaller group of women who is a published martial art writer.

I have worked very hard, and nothing has been handed to me. Time and effort yield powerful results for everyone. Entering a male dominated world and infiltrating from every direction seems like a hearty dose of power to most people, but to me, it is a natural progression of who I am.

Power is in your hands, too. If you have a dream or a goal, there is only one way to get there. The main step is to try. You may fail along the way, but each failure becomes a positive, because it thrusts you forward, teaches you what not to do, and steers you in the right direction.

Just like many other people, I was afraid to try. When you feel uncomfortable, it is a natural response. I did not want others to know that I was going out on a limb by trying a martial art. I was not sure if I would hold up or crack under the pressure.

I have tried many things during my life, including ways to make more money, get in shape, eat better, be a better person, learn more, and improve my life. In every category, I have failed miserably at one time or another. It does not matter how many failures you have, because all you need is one success amongst all the failures for powerful results.

If you follow through on your dreams and goals, at some point you will reap the reward. This thoughtful acceptance and acknowledgement of your efforts is a strong black belt approach, and truly powerful.

I also implement powerful patience. No one achieves a black belt in a day, a week, a month, or maybe even years. If you want results, you must be patient in all facets of your life. It may take a long time, but it will be worth it. Strive to be consistent with your goals and your vision, because success needs breeding.

Ideas and actions must come together in a myriad of ways until the right combination adheres. You can start a project today, and it is wonderful if you achieve immediate success. Chances are, however, that you will need some time to formulate the right mix of ingredients for success.

Through my empowerment in martial arts, commanding decisions are a part of my everyday life. To engage power, start by asking yourself, "Does this feel right?" when deciding. Make a list of pros and cons. Study and weigh each factor. Does this decision have more pros than cons? Does it fit with your goals? Does it make sense based on your lifestyle? Does it allow you to continue your current responsibilities? If you answer honestly, your decision will surface.

I have made many decisions in my life, some better than others. My martial art training taught me how important it is to apply these criteria. I would have never become a black belt if I did not ask myself some of these questions along the way.

I also learned that if an idea or option does not feel right, it probably is not. Not being very positive in my younger years was not a good decision. I wasted a lot of time with negative energy and did not feel particularly happy or energetic. Deciding to learn a martial art was a great decision. If I look back and apply the questions I have just outlined to my martial arts experiences, I can confidently respond, "Yes!" to each.

If you cannot negotiate a decision or opportunity to your terms, move on. Another opportunity will come your way. As a woman, I had to decide if I could live up to the responsibility of being a female martial artist. There is a stigma that confirms that I have what it takes to be a powerful force. Power grows quietly like a wind, gets stronger without warning. Through practice, power never wanes.

If I had not learned a martial art, I probably would still be searching for my power. I would still be wondering what I was put on this earth to do. I heard a clear calling to practice, and later, to share with others how my martial art has influenced and molded me into who I am as a woman.

If you want to grow, stop massaging the surface, and look beneath to your true desires and meaning. That is where personal power grows and it is how you can avoid becoming stagnant.

Have you ever seen an older person who stopped changing his wardrobe years ago? He still wears the same shirts that have hung in his closet all these years. Time stopped. He was unable to move forward or to adapt.

You cannot stay the same either, if you want to live a powerful life. Do not let time stop, and do not settle into thinking that you cannot do more. No matter your age or lot in life, you have great potential to make each day count, to excel, and to hone the power. This is the martial art way.

Recently, as I taught a few martial art classes, I looked around at the students, youngest to oldest, and saw proof of each student's potential. Power exists when practice and perseverance come together. When you experience this, it feels as natural as the air around you.

As a martial arts woman who has achieved her own goals, I can confirm that whatever your goals, aspirations, or desires are, you can achieve power too. Take initiative, bring forth a martial art spirit, and start today. Face your challenges head on, try your best, and when you turn your failures into success, you will create true and practical power. If you push through boundaries, you will be stronger for it, but it takes effort and commitment.

Martial arts allowed me to make powerful choices. Good decisions yield powerful results. The martial art woman learns to develop these decision-making skills early on in her practice, and she quietly carries them wherever she goes. Her mindset, ambitions, and everyday experiences, push her ahead in the power category because she is in control of her life.

If you and I could share our positive power, the world would be better for it. The truth is that you and I have all the power we need; we just need to proclaim it. Thanks to martial arts, I am a powerful woman, and I am proud of it.

The question isn't who is going to let me; it's who is going to stop me.

Ayn Rand

The Myths of Me
Andrea Harkins

Through my practice, I have carved out a niche, and a special place in all of history, just by being a female martial artist. I cannot think of anything else that so immediately awards me the distinction of being an interesting and accomplished woman.

I have trained for a long time, and many people only know me as Sensei Andrea. People outside the dojo have different assumptions about me, though, based solely on my role as a martial artist. Most of these assumptions are not accurate and are generally applied to female martial artists across the board. I am going to debunk a few of these myths, finally.

The first myth is that I am interested in kicking, flipping, or controlling someone. I know that sounds very exciting and very Hollywood. I cannot deny that in a true need-to-save-myself scenario, I could manage all of this, but it is not something I think of doing, just because I am a female martial artist.

I am a trained practitioner, but along with that, I am a mom, a wife, an employee, a volunteer, and many other things. My superpowers are always charged, but rarely used except in practice mode.

I do not walk down the street with the intent of blasting any potential assailant, nor do I dream of physically fighting the bad people. I can if I must. I will fight, and battle, and beat them if my life depends on it, but I am not out to save the world with my bravery. I really would rather run the other way.

As a female martial artist, I am also not some supermodel athlete or in peak physical condition. I work out several times a week and lift weights, but I am no twenty-something, MMA, super fighter in the ring.

I have managed to carve out some good muscle tone, and I still enjoy a good aerobic workout. I am a dynamo and determined. Not everyone, including me, can measure up to some of those amazing female MMA practitioners and fighters, but I have my own set of positive attributes.

Next, I did not stop at a second-degree black belt because I could not rank higher. With my years of experience teaching, writing for a major martial arts magazine, and owning my own martial art program, I could slap another stripe around my belt as easily as anyone could. That is not about who I am.

A while ago, I wanted to train toward my third degree. The physical challenge would be doable, but by the time politics, favors and other silly things were revealed, I decided that being a female role model with only two stripes on my belt was just as effective as being a female role model with five stripes.

No student ever asks when I am testing next, or what my rank is. It does not matter, because being a role model is about more than a belt. It is about being a woman who has achieved success on many levels, including in a typically male dominated world, and that on its own, has merit.

Today, I am actively training, but not necessarily for a higher degree. I am doing it for me. If I earn a higher rank, that is icing on the cake. I am working on it because it is the right thing to do, not because someone owes me a favor, or because I feel inferior about who I am. I am not going to play the "reciprocate a favor" game, or engage in any politics to earn it.

Another myth is that I frequently practice at home. You would think that with black belts in the family, and martial art equipment at home, that I practice at home a lot. Even with a second-degree black belt husband, and two black belt children, I do not usually even have time to bow when I walk in my front door. Practicing at home is a luxury, when it does happen.

I also do not take every opportunity I can, to display my cool moves on some poor, unsuspecting guy in class, just to exhibit my womanly power. While on some occasions, I wish I could do that, my martial art focus is more about teaching than proving myself. I have a responsibility to make sure my students are learning something. It is not about ego.

I am also not into any bizarre behaviors just because I am a female martial artist! I am not a sexy villain in some romance novel. I know being a martial art woman has an element of intrigue, but if you want a realistic description of me, hardworking and committed to helping others, are probably more accurate.

I do not have a special personality because I am a martial artist. I am who I am. I do sport some awesome uniforms with my black belt, and I do not mind standing in front of a camera to film some motivational talks. Make me who you want, but in my opinion, a super high achiever is what tops the list.

Finally, I am as intense in life as I am in training. Combining my capabilities and my desire for excellence is what I do best. I try to take care of myself by living life in moderation and exercising. While I strive to be the best I can be, in my opinion, the art outweighs the sport.

I did not take a martial art to make a statement, create a strong womanly persona, or even to learn to be empowered. If anyone takes it for these reasons, they are the wrong reasons. A martial art has its own meaning. You do not have to create a meaning for it. A woman will naturally become more confident through her practice. While the transformation is quite magical, it is through hard and diligent effort, not magic, that the female martial artist finds empowerment.

I want to share what I have learned because the world needs it. Martial arts have made me a healthier person, and I have fostered an excellent motivational thought process in my life because of them.

I confess, being a female martial artist is more special than I ever imagined. It has helped me to grow as a person and tap into talents that I had never previously recognized. I am a role model because of my actions. I am an independent thinker and, at times, courageous. There is no myth to be broken. My passion and presence are two parts of me that no one can deny.

Who you decide I am is up to you, but the biggest misconception that I want to address is that I have always had a courageous and dedicated spirit and an unwavering vision. The truth is, martial arts made me who I am today and not the other way around.

Believe you can and you're halfway there.
Theodore Roosevelt

LOVE & COMMITMENT

Too many of us are not living our dreams because we are living our fears.
Les Brown

The Martial Art Promise
Andrea Harkins

A woman makes promises every day. She promises to be a caring daughter, a good wife or partner, a loving mother, a reliable sister, and a meaningful friend. She is often a caretaker and a woman of sacrifice.

Just by her nature, she makes many promises. Think of your own mother, her loving relationship, and how important her many compromises and sacrifices have been for you. If not a mother, then some other important woman in your life, who has helped you to develop into the person you are today.

I have four children and my promise is to always love them fully, take care of them, and make sure they have what they need, even if it means sacrifice for me. I am a daughter and with that is the promise of respect and appreciation for my mother. I am a wife and that involves its own set of loving obligations.

A martial art is a personal promise that I make to myself. It is a refreshing, uplifting, and encouraging diversion from daily life, and helps me to cope with all the tasks, and responsibilities that I have in my other roles.

The woman who makes the martial art promise can put all her other promises aside, perhaps for an hour or two a week, to seek discovery of her spirit. When she is in class, she does not have to think about anything, except her own learning of the techniques and skills presented.

My martial art promise to myself is a focus that goes inward and is philosophical, which is a drastic change from how and what I think in some of my other roles. Typically, there is no time in class to think about what needs completion at home or at work. It is my chance, my personal promise of self-development, and I try to make it a promise not easily broken.

I am renewed because this promise helps me to establish who I am, and who I want to be. Beneath the surface of my everyday character and demeanor, is a woman warrior who hopes to find new energy, fulfillment, and confidence. My practice is a mental retreat and the one place where I can logically face my fears, regrets, worries, and insecurities, and diligently work through each one.

Like the thickest fiber of a rope, the martial art promise winds its way through a woman's life. She starts to realize that her commitments connect with varying degrees of priority. The martial art promise strengthens every aspect and helps her to develop a strong and positive mindset in all facets of her life.

Once this promise takes root, the martial art woman will never need to resort to negativity or to being a victim again, without examining better alternatives. Her martial art promise holds the key to breaking mental barriers and obstacles.

Through this promise, truths that are more powerful are revealed. The martial art woman learns that every question has an answer, and every obstacle has a solution. She faces mental and physical barriers with intent. She learns to defend against negativity, but also against more literal, physical attacks, because the promise is not just to enrich her life, but to defend.

I have never been attacked. Even though I am well trained, it still scares me. That is why a woman must commit to this promise. Her defense must become second nature for it to be valid. She needs to know as much as possible to save herself and to safeguard her other promises.

When the martial art woman makes this promise to herself, a continuum begins. It affects all that she does, inside and outside the dojo. There should be no hesitation and no looking back. Forward moving, ever ready and committed, this promise is worth it.

Whatever gaps are missing, and any areas of weakness that a woman has will strengthen through her ongoing martial art promise. Her martial art enhances all her other roles and all her other actions. When she partakes in this mindset she knows, without a doubt, that it is the most ambitious and crucial promise that she can ever make.

Marriage to Martial Arts
Andrea Harkins

Marriage is an excellent correlation to my relationship with martial arts. Through the initial courtship phase, the engagement, and the ultimate commitment of black belt, this martial art relationship is supposed to last.

I view my martial art practice as a personal relationship. It is where I can go to shed my frustrations or enjoy a peaceful moment. Whatever emotion I have, I can improve or celebrate it through this relationship, either through mindful reflection or a physical hammering out of techniques and skills.

Like any valued relationship, my martial art requires frequent communication through practice and patience to keep it strong. I need to always understand how it enhances my life and be appreciative of it. Like a marriage, there is a deep bond, and I feel more fulfilled than I would if it were not a part of my life.

For many women, the martial art relationship initially helps to destroy personal fears, abuses, or worries. What woman does not want to feel safer, or at least have some idea of what to do when the hairs rise on the back of her neck in dreadful anticipation? What can she do if an attack is imminent?

This relationship is multi-faceted. Self-growth, self-defense, and a myriad of other reasons, make this marriage to martial arts purposeful and multi-dimensional. The beginning of the martial art relationship is like dating. It does not require a long-term commitment, but there are no long-term benefits, either. In the beginning, a woman must decide if this is important and right for her. When guiding the direction of her practice, she should consider personal goals.

The first day of class is like a blind date. It is not always love at first sight. For me, it was a time when I questioned myself. It is easy to think that you do not have what it takes when watching experienced martial art students, but even for them, this kind of relationship took a long time to flourish.

Before a woman commits, she seeks answers of all kinds. Am I good enough? Can I overcome confidence issues? Will this be too difficult? How compatible is this with my life and my goals? If she decides that a martial art is a suitable companion, she moves forward to advance through the belt levels and the ranks, which effectively translates into personal excellence elsewhere in her life.

Over time, her training shakes her through physical fitness, and she must dig deep for stamina. A piece of herself that she has never seen before will reveal. This is the courtship of self; now she begins to establish martial artistry in her life.

Her initial practice emerges into something more. She soon becomes a full-fledged practitioner and is consistent and reliable in her commitment. In this engagement phase, she also becomes more confident and eventually assumes a leadership role. When a man enters class with a furrowed brow because he notices a woman is his instructor, she takes it all in stride, and proceeds, unwavering in her confidence and empowered with her knowledge.

The engagement phase can last for a long time. It is a time when she notices the good and the bad. She will start to see some discrepancies in other martial artists and learn a few things about politics that she never expected. She will see some of the flaws that exist and notice how ego or superiority define others. She will ask herself if she can remain, for better or for worse.

She chooses to progress forward, because she knows that she can make a difference. She achieves belts, awards, and certificates. She takes tests and competes. Martial arts become a part of everything she does. The bond is deep.

The day will come when she earns her black belt, and her instructor gingerly ties it around her waist. When she sees it for the first time, she is ecstatic. She realizes that the first day of class, so long ago, was not the beginning of her journey after all.

I have been married to my husband as long as I have been married to martial arts. I can line these two marriages up side by side and see correlations. The day we were married started our married life, just as the day I received my black belt started the beginning of my true martial art journey.

My martial art conviction has strengthened over time, and as in any relationship, it has peaks and valleys. Like all the black belts before me, I progressed through the steps of this martial art relationship, first with skepticism, then infatuation, and then conviction.

In my marriage, my wedding ring is a sacred symbol of my commitment. In my martial art, my black belt is a sacred symbol of who I am as a martial art woman.

You may wonder if I plan to practice a martial art forever. I believe that even if there comes a day when I cannot perform the physical skills, I will always be devoted to the martial art mindset. The real question is, do I take this martial art to heart? Do I commit? The answer will not surprise you. I do!

My Married Martial Arts Life
Jackie Bradbury

My husband and I are unusual, because we are both active and passionate about martial arts. We were married 16 years before we stepped onto a mat. He started his training about 6 months before I did, but we are now the same rank in our primary art, Presas Arnis, and we both pursue our own martial arts interests outside of our primary art. I study Kobudo, while he studies Goju-Shorei weapons and trains with Hock Hochheim's organization.

I know a few couples, who practice martial arts together, but typically, they met in martial arts and married later, or the husband was practicing first, and then the wife joined. It is rare to find couples who were married then started their journey together. Our journey in martial arts, just as in our journey in marriage, is together.

Training together is great because I get to spend a lot of time with my husband doing what we both love. It is ideal because he has different talents and strengths than I do, and we complement each other well. A married martial art life takes some effort to work. We have learned how to achieve happiness in both, through a few simple lessons.

First, we keep our marital relationship off the mats. Even though we have been married 25 years, you would not be able to tell during practice, if you did not already know. When he does something awesome in class, I keep the feedback for when we are alone, and not with the other students. We keep it professional, like in a workplace.

We also know how to coach each other. This is something we had to learn. Since day one, our marriage has been one of equality and partnership. One being a higher rank than the other did not work well, and listening to my husband talk to me as if I were a lower ranked stranger, was irritating, and made me resentful. The truth is that he did outrank me, so we had to learn how to coach each other without being condescending.

This is especially important now that we are the same rank. If we teach each other something, we try to speak respectfully. This allows us to be better partners and coaches to other people, too.

We are always each other's biggest fan. I make a point of complimenting him, even when he is not around. I support him in his ideas and in his martial art practice. I share his successes and his failures, and he does the same for me. It is a healthy marriage because we apply martial art principles to it.

There are many advantages to training together. We never run out of topics to discuss. We try new martial art techniques together. We go to the garage dojo and practice with each other.

We always have a training partner, and we can always talk the other into trying a technique on which we want to work. Neither of us likes to be wrong about a technique. We can get into debates over this, and neither of us emerges the winner.

When we want to purchase a martial art item, we rarely have to justify it to the other. It is obvious when I need a new gi, or a weapon, and I completely understand why he wants to purchase a banner of his martial art to hang in our garage dojo.

These aspects of our martial art marriage are great. There are some downsides; however, scheduling is an especially difficult task. Now that we study together and separately, trying to manage the family schedule is difficult. Childcare is difficult to find, and the solutions are sometimes less than ideal.

Now that our youngest is old enough to sit on the sidelines, and read or color, it is more convenient. Our older daughter is old enough to watch my youngest now and then, but it does not always work out for longer events, like seminars or boot camps. Sometimes it means one of us gets to go to the martial arts event, and the other stays home.

This is our married martial arts life. We have learned to make it work by practicing a martial art and practicing mutual respect. This is how my husband and I keep it working after training together for seven of our twenty-five years of marriage.

Destined to Die
Andrea Harkins

Starting a family was the perfect time for me to practice the mindset and discipline that I had learned in martial arts. You can apply what you learn in the dojang to life. You become better prepared to overcome the obstacles that may arise in life through your mindful practice of a martial art, although that does not mean obstacles are easier to overcome. It means that you fight harder to overcome them.

When I got married in 1988, I was twenty-five years old and had my entire married life ahead of me. After waiting six years to have our first child, I finally became pregnant in 1993. It was an exciting time. I knew that bringing a new child into the world would be an amazing experience.

That is what I thought, until I experienced a miscarriage. It was devastating. No matter what anyone says, it hurts. They can say, "You will get pregnant again," or "The same thing happened to me," or "Hang in there," but none of that makes sense at the time.

Martial arts helped me recover both mentally and physically. I was certain that one obstacle did not mean that I should give up, or that I was destined to be childless. During this difficult time, the only thing that made any semblance of sense was what I had learned in martial arts.

I knew from sparring, that even if you do everything right, you sometimes still lose. I learned from katas that even if the direction feels wrong, it could still be right. I understood that the mind could focus with the precision of a blade, if you call upon it. Using these principles, I moved forward from my first miscarriage, to a healthy pregnancy, and a beautiful child.

I was not destined to have an easy time during my childbearing years, however. There were thorny barriers and difficult emotions on my road to having more children. There were heartbreaking times, but with a strong sense of perseverance, I continued to move forward. I managed through another miscarriage, which was again difficult, but nothing prepared me for the pregnancy that pushed me to my absolute limit.

This pregnancy pulled out all the punches. It knocked me down in several ways. It forced me to use the most intimate, determined, and devoted aspects of my martial arts training and mindset. In my fifth month of pregnancy, the doctors told me that my baby was destined to die.

It all started with a few minor complications. Being of advanced maternal age, and because I had the history of miscarrying, I went to the doctor with my concerns. Based on my history of prior pregnancy issues, they sent me immediately to the Emergency Room as a precaution.

I did not know that my life would change forever on that day. I had no idea that I would enter the hospital and not leave again for six long weeks.

There was no chance to pack the toothbrush or toothpaste, and no opportunity to prepare for what was about to happen. I was in premature labor.

The doctor who admitted me said there was little chance that I could save this pregnancy. I took a medication to try to stop the labor. It gave me double vision and a tremendous headache. Family from out of town were visiting, and came to the hospital to visit me. They ordered some ice and placed it on my forehead because of the tremendous headache the medicine caused.

Enough medication put the labor to rest temporarily, while everyone tried to think of how to handle the situation. Medical staff and specialists entered my room every few hours, with their very detailed medical explanation and heart-wrenching details of my child's impending death. An emergency surgery still did not increase the odds of my baby's survival. I was on strict bedrest, and my hospital bed was inverted so my feet higher than my head, to not put pressure on the baby's position.

If ever a martial art mindset meant anything, it was then. I wondered every single day, when the moment would come that my labor would proceed, and I would lose my child. I always knew that I might need to use my martial art to save a life, but I never expected it would be like this. I always thought that if I had to save a life it would be in a physical altercation, not a mental one.

"This baby will not survive," were the only words that I ever heard in the hospital, yet I felt something completely different. At 24 weeks, I could feel the baby moving. Nothing any doctor could ever say could change that. The doctors warned me that the flutters in my stomach could not stop this from happening. They wanted me to be prepared and understand the tremendous disappointment I was about to endure.

The whole ordeal required strict bedrest. I had sponge baths in bed, and stitched needlepoint flat on my back. I rested, but uncomfortably. I looked out the window. I prayed and cried a lot, too. Even worse, I was more scared than I have ever been. I could only equate it to a fight with an opponent twice my size. When I imagined the fight in my head, I knew that I could win that fight if my technique and training were impeccable. Belief, perseverance, and a fighting attitude were what mattered.

I had personal faith and my martial art as two guiding forces. I had to do everything that I possibly could to keep this child. I could not give up. My intense martial art mindset focused me, and I was unwavering. While others may have started to believe that the end was near, I stayed mentally strong and kept pushing through. I hoped that each moment that passed would make a difference. I needed to keep death from knocking at my baby's door.

I never gave up. I told the doctors that I would stand on my head 24/7, if that would help and I meant it. That was my martial art mindset. I was willing to do the impossible. Training taught me to never listen to "I can't" and always focus on "I can."

Days turned into weeks and strangely enough, I started to settle into a routine consisting of watching television and visits from my mother, husband, and kids. I faced hours upon hours of nothingness and loneliness.

It is easy for fear to creep in when you have a lot of time on your hands, and you are facing impending doom. Your mind wants to sway to the negative. You feel like throwing your hands up and proclaiming, "Fine, I give up," and yet you must not. It is like trying to break a board that feels too thick for a technique. If you do not believe in yourself, there is absolutely no chance you can ever break through.

If I left it to medical staff, I would have let go and given up. The doctors and nurses had concern for me, but were certain that my baby's life was over.

One day, a technician took an ultrasound and told me it looked worse than before. To me, this meant that my baby's life was ending. I sobbed. Later, the doctor came in only to tell me that the technician was incorrect, nothing had changed.

This was a turning point for me. This moment helped me finally make my own conclusions. I decided to believe what my martial mind was telling me. As unique as a martial art is to each practitioner, so is a mother's love for her child. The emotional rollercoaster ride was crazy. I finally decided to do the one thing that would give me a fighting chance. I would never listen to any of them again. I would only listen to the cunning fighter's voice inside my head that knew there was only one way to win.

Time was on hold. Would this pregnancy give me an angel or a child? The choice was beyond my control, but how I handled it was not. I chose to listen to myself and to allow my martial art life philosophies to defend against the medical professionals' unintentional threats against my baby's life. I shut out anything negative and focused on my positive energy.

I had given up on things in my life before, but not this. Martial arts were my saving grace. I needed the ability to control my emotions and stay focused and centered. My prior years of training gave me that edge. I had to find energy, a chi of some sort, to convince my mental and physical health to keep pace with my positive thoughts. I knew what it meant to accomplish something monumental. I was, after all, a second-degree black belt. Martial arts, in their own way, prepared me for this very moment.

I began to apply what I had learned from martial arts to help me overcome this enormous stress and burden. I closed my eyes and performed every kata in my mind. I imagined myself the victorious winner of a sparring match. I slowed my breathing to a very thoughtful, steady pace to visualize health, peace, and a baby in my arms. If I could have let out a loud yell, or kiai, I would have.

In my loneliness, I recalled the many times in my martial art when I had to step up my game to succeed. It was not that difficult to throw someone, but being thrown and falling the right way, took practice. In class, I had to learn to flip and fall without hurting myself. My whole life was flipping over, and I had to figure out how to fall without hurting myself.

Doctors wanted me to give up and told me that I was hoping for something unrealistic, so I tried harder. My martial art perseverance bolstered me, and years of training reminded my body to follow my mind. Like my martial art accomplishments, I set high expectations knowing it was either pass or fail.

When something surreal happens in your life, you suddenly cannot think about anything else. My whole life funneled into one unexpected, traumatic moment and stopped. Time felt like it stood still, yet the weeks of hospitalization continued. Not knowing the outcome of a completely unexpected situation, one thrust upon you in an instant, is incredibly difficult to handle.

In this life-changing adventure, when I carried the son who was destined to die, I changed the lives of nurses and doctors who prayed with me, and I re-routed my own delicate mentality to fight harder than I have ever fought before. I could not have fought harder if I was in a ring, or facing the largest assailant on earth.

I do believe that things happen for a reason, but I also believe that what the mind thinks can sway even the most negative, discouraging personal disasters from happening. The moment I decided to stop listening to others and apply my martial art mindset and awareness was the moment I started to save my child's life.

After months of hospital stays and bed rest at home, I arrived at the hospital again on February 10, 2001 to deliver my baby, full term. I had won, and I felt as victorious as a champion did. Did my martial arts mindset save him? Was it my faith? I believe that the positive strengths allowed me to seek the truth and not back down.

There are so many life lessons from this event. Whatever challenges you face in your life, there are always two tracks to follow. Path one consists of insecurities, doubts, fears, and the inability to discern what is true and right for you. Path two has hope. With a martial art mindset, you can aspire to overcome even the most dreadful proclamations. The martial arts woman will never accept "destined to die" at face value. She will never allow negativity to be the only option.

This story is not about superpowers, and certainly, in some cases, babies simply do not make it on earth, but find their way to Heaven on the short track. You never know if your burdens are a test to determine how strong you really are. One day, you may need to use your martial heart without knowing how things will work out.

You can and should apply a martial art mindset to every aspect of life. This mindset could mean the difference between giving up, or in believing when it really matters. Most importantly, it could mean the difference between life and death.

Hateshinai Zanshin – Perpetual Vigilance
Sama Bellomo

Still in bed, not having moved yet, I start with my head and work my way down, taking inventory of how my body has contorted during the night, a move I call "undo the pretzel." I plan to align my bones back into the shape of a human being, carefully breathing to keep the pain under control.

Some of my joints have dislocated during the night. My forearms have snuck out from inside their sleeping splints. My fingers are cranky. The ring splints that hold their bones in place have become tight from the night's swelling. From the moment I wake up, I remember that my body is not going to work like other people's bodies. I am literally falling apart at every joint.

I am not sure if it is safe to yawn, or if my jaw will dislocate and cause a headache that will last the rest of the day. I press my tongue to the roof of my mouth trying to stabilize my jaw and take a breath. It works, and I am ready to move.

Pretzel undone, my next step is to pump my ankles. Once I pop them back into place, the ligaments snap back to where they belong, to move blood to my brain. This way, when I sit up, I will not black out. I also do pelvic tilts and other isometric exercises to wake up my body, while making a list of what braces I will need for the day, based on what hurts the most. It is a happy time, because if I have gotten to this point, I am going to be able to get up and start my day.

I have splints, pain creams and meds for every joint and a workable layman understanding of anatomy and physiology. Not everyone gets this far, and those who do will not always be able to stay at this functional level. Today, I can do it.

I live with Ehlers-Danlos Syndrome. Among other things, this genetic deficiency of collagen means that any of my joints can dislocate at any time. Without collagen, the body's most abundant protein, my skin connects poorly to me. I cannot regulate my blood pressure, heart rate, or body temperature internally (Dysautonomia). My digestive tract is on its way to paralysis, and I am in pain all the time.

At the time of this writing, I am 33 years old with a college degree, a full-time job, and enough friends to pave a path for miles and miles. Many people with symptoms as severe as mine have had to let go of their dreams and lifestyles. Rather than consider myself unlucky for the problems I face, I fancy myself a lucky duck for having survived. My dojo accepts me how I am, which helps me accept myself. I have karate in two hours, starting at 8:00 a.m. on this Saturday morning.

When class begins, we will kneel in mokuso, silent contemplation, but I have thoughts that need my attention sooner. Every morning, I deliberately give thanks with two full breaths. I have plenty of time with my thoughts because my lungs have an unusually high capacity. Breathing in, I give thanks to God, enjoying how my faith nourishes me. Breathing out, I give thanks to myself, because I work hard to be as well as possible. Breathing in, I give thanks to the medical teams that keep me well. Breathing out, I am thankful to those who walk beside me in life.

Two full breaths wake me up, and I am ready to take on the day's adventures. It is time to get up! Sitting up is easier now that my occupational therapist installed a bar on the side of my bed that helps me pull myself up. It even has a pocket on it where I keep water, tissues, as-needed meds, pain cream, and whatever else gets me through the night.

It feels good to grab the bar and think about how I have adequate access to medical care, where it was not always that way, and may not always be the case. It hurts that not all the people who need medical care will ever get it. Practicing martial arts lends itself to injuries, and people with astronomical medical bills generally avoid risk.

Having a disability limits independence, and while I have learned to let myself have support, I never want to fear being alone. Because I practice karate, I am no longer afraid that a walk in the city in my wheelchair will make me an easy target. Sensei taught me, "If somebody wants to hurt you, you want to make it very hard for them."

I am not afraid of pain because it is a part of my daily life, which gives me a small advantage in training. Feet on the floor, I stand up. Bearing weight is the only way to know if the bones of my feet are where they belong, so I am glad I have two feet, in case I need to lift one up and adjust it right away. A few cracks and pops click the assembly into place, and I am satisfied with my efforts to put myself together.

The bones of my hands and feet are the loosest, but they still work well enough for me to walk and steady myself. I take a few cautious steps and discover that I am going to be fine. My visual field is intact, I can think clearly, I can feel my legs, and just for good measure, I smile because I do not have a toothache.

I think my blood pressure is going to remain stable on my walk to the bathroom, but I keep my knees slightly bent and lean backward, because I've practiced break falls on the mat and I'm not so afraid of cracking my head open anymore. I still have relative control of my bowel and bladder, and even though I have been up a half-dozen times throughout the night, I do not dawdle. Today could be that day.

Collagen is the sponge that holds water in the body. Without it, chronic dehydration is a life-threatening problem that does not take long to become severe. Five years ago, I became dependent on IV fluids to keep my blood pressure high enough to keep me conscious. I could no longer keep fluids down by drinking water. Dysphagia finally made me choke easily, and problems of low smooth muscle tone in my digestive organs made reflux a constant problem.

Three years ago, I began resisting this IV treatment because every IV needle stick sent my body into shock from the pain. Nurses packed my head and shoulders in ice while trying to access my veins through my arms. My skin is loose, like the skin on a shar pei puppy. My veins are thin and dehydrated, rolling and bursting easily. Three times a week, I sat for nine hours a day in the nurses' station, tethered to an IV pole.

Exercise was not in the equation and sitting up was barely possible. My skin is too loose for a PICC line, so I endured the needle sticks, shock, tears, and infusions upon each visit. Nurses cried with me as they watched me struggle through the pain, as they attempted to stick a vein. Those days are over.

Now, there is a port-a-cath in my chest giving me direct access to my heart via my jugular vein, and I push a fresh, sterile needle into it. My port (fondly nicknamed "Portholomew") is how I get enough IV saline into my heart to keep my blood volume and blood pressure up while I exercise, allowing me to stay conscious. I grab a 2-litre bag of saline from the fridge and run the tubing through my pump, then drop the assembly into my backpack, which I will don as soon as I connect the line to my port and start the pump.

I feel good about my pump because it has given me my life back. I no longer spend time at nursing stations, or dragging IV poles around. Three years ago, I got my port implanted, and that is when my martial art life began.

Once I had my port, no one knew how many quality years I had left to live, and for my mental health, I decided to pursue my dream of practicing karate. Getting started was the hardest part of following a dream. No dojo would accept me, afraid of the liability.

Two months after I gave up on my search, I decided to give it one more try. I noticed a man at the grocery store at the salad bar. He looked svelte and strong, and wore a sweatshirt that bore the words, "Discipline, Strength, and Humility." I asked if he was a karate instructor, and he said he was.

I told him briefly about Ehlers-Danlos Syndrome and Dysautonomia, and told him that I had been having trouble pursuing my dream of learning karate. He handed me his card and told me to come at 8:00 a.m. on Saturday. On Saturday morning, I arrived at 7:40 a.m. He said, "I did not think you would show up."

Toothpaste bubbles up under my tongue and it feels good to have found a product that will not break down the skin inside my mouth. I am looking forward to breakfast because I think it is going to stay down today, if I can just remember to take my medications before I take my first bite to keep the food moving in the right direction. Now that my fluids are running, I will feel better before too long. I have a positive attitude, but I am still in pain. The nausea will double me over if I let it overpower me.

I swallow my medicines, 11 pills for the morning, and eat some egg whites loaded with Himalayan pink salt to get my blood pressure up. I have a good sense of how my joints are working. My body is nourished, and I have met most of my medical needs for the next hour. My medical life is so complex, that I refuse to let the rest of my life get as complicated. In my commitment to simplicity, it is time to relax with tea.

The tea is hot, and I am encouraged by being able to drink it. I take careful sips and think about my tube-fed friends whose dysphagia is too far along for them to enjoy this simple pleasure. I deliberately ignore the odds that I will join them eventually. This one's for them, I think to myself. Salut. To their health. Penza lu male, si vuo lu bene is a Sicilian proverb, to think of the worst if you want the best.

The strong Jasmine essence in this tea will taste better than the egg, should it come back up while I am exercising this morning. I am planning. For as yucky a thought as it is, at least I will not have the taste of eggs on my breath while I am trying to execute roundhouse kicks.

It feels comforting to relax. Saturday morning is my favorite karate day, and this sky-high level of function in my body is rare. I listen to the panting of my IV pump and feel the cool fluids begin to lower my body temperature. My meds and breakfast are staying down, and fortunately, my bones are where they belong. I sit neatly, folded on a cinnamon red sofa with a sandy beige blanket comforting my feet, which get cold soon when fluids are running.

This is a mandatory rest time after the morning routine. Without it, my muscles fatigue and my joints will begin to fall apart. In addition to their normal job of moving my bones, my muscles do the work that my tendons and ligaments cannot do without collagen, joints together and stabilize me.

On this morning, I meet my body's needs, and this is my time! I collect my thoughts, breathe mindfully, and make some notes in a notebook. Today, my hands can hold the pen, and it feels empowering to write. This is the time to take care of my thoughts and feelings. It is the quiet hour, when I adjust my attitude. I am cautiously excited to be this far along in my day, without any major issues. I am excited to know that in another hour I will be at the dojo, where I am my happiest!

My mind wanders to who will be there, and how well I will be able to hold my balance during warm-ups. My hips seem to be staying in their sockets today. The next time I am still, it will be only for a moment while we open the class with our dojokun, our dojo's benediction:

Through discipline, strength, and humility
I will strive to bring out the best in myself and others.
I will use common sense before self-defense,
And never be abusive or offensive.
I will strive to have patience, kindness, gentleness, and self-control.
Warriors of Grace Karate Dojokun, by Sensei Tony Ferrer (used with permission)

I put on my fresh, white gi while I am still at home because it is hard for me to get dressed, and it takes a long time. My classmates will drive to the dojo in street clothes and change when they arrive, but it helps me to be in my own environment where I can change more slowly and safely. I am as careful as I can be to not brush up against anything dirty once I am dressed. My gi is one of the most important garments I own.

Because my bones are loose, I lean against walls as I walk, to keep track of my body's orientation and direction. Time in my gi is a chance to work on my body's ability to know where it is in space. With trust in myself, I will walk mindfully and not fall over.

This is one of many times in my day where I tell myself that I'll just have to have a little mercy if it doesn't go as planned. The Suriashi drills on the flat and forgiving dojo floor have helped tremendously with my footwork. I let myself move, mindful of my delicate balance, rather than fearful of losing it. Sensei has taught me well, and every careful step is a tiny nod of thanks in his direction.

My IV backpack is running and ready to go. My karate bag has a side pocket loaded with IV anti-emetics vials, syringes and needles, drinking water, saline, IV pump tubing, extra adhesives, and alcohol wipes. The other side pocket holds my emergency care document. The same pocket has extra pain meds and pain creams.

There is sports tape and scissors for any quick joint fixes, and a bunch of other incidentals. The front pocket carries toothpaste and a toothbrush, as well as other toiletries, because my karate bag doubles as a hospital bag, in case I end up staying. The bag's main compartment holds raggedy workout clothes that people usually stow in their gym bags.

Most importantly, my obi is in my karate bag. My belt is one of the most valuable items I own, and it is purple with a black stripe. Three more belts before black in Goju Ryu karate. It is a heavy thought, and I put it out of my head straight away, to protect myself from the worry of getting too sick to continue. Mindfulness helps me through.

In this moment, I am happy to be at a 4-kyu belt level, and I am looking forward to this morning's opportunity to do my best. I bid goodbye to my two kittens and carry all my treasures to the car. With sunglasses on and splints holding my thumbs on, I grip the steering wheel and head to the dojo.

Because I cannot regulate my body temperature, fresh air is a rare commodity. If I go outside in the sun, I risk passing out and dehydrating. The weather is cool for this time of year and I am glad to drive with the windows down, singing at the top of my lungs. My training in opera serves as a great warm-up method, because I open my lungs on the way to the dojo, which will help later with consciousness and breathing through pain.

Today, I will surely be practicing Sanchin kata, the Three Battles form to challenge one's body, mind, and spirit. Sanchin is a series of movements made with all muscles contracted, with breath forcefully blasting through one's body. It is a practice at slow and controlled mastery of one's physical, intellectual, and emotional focus.

Most days I black out and throw up. Nobody gives me a hard time when I step out to take care of myself. Today, I am ready to take on Sanchin, knowing that it makes me steadier each time I do it. I will learn about my body's needs and abilities, and my stamina will increase because of my effort. With Ehlers-Danlos Syndrome, planning and problem solving govern much of every day.

Like the kata, success is about balance. Complementary to balance, zanshin is the concept of residual mindfulness and of continued awareness, even after a conflict has ended. Vigilance is an essential component to life with a chronic illness. I am always on the lookout for what may go wrong, but also for what may go better. On either occasion, I aim to be ready.

Although I feel good in the moment, I park in the accessible spot in front of the dojo, in case I am not able to walk out of the dojo unassisted, or in case I need someone to fetch my crutches. Parking near the door also reduces my risk of falling on uneven pavement, and reduces my exposure to temperature changes that can make me black out.

I rehearse these accommodations in my head to remind myself that they are legitimate reasons. I have my reasons ready in case anyone challenges me for parking in an accessible spot, because I do not look like I have a soul-crushing genetic disorder. Loading up my shoulders with my IV bag and my karate bag, I take a deep breath of morning air before pulling the door open.

I am a morning person in a world where most people are not, and I am excited to have made it to the dojo. On the other side of this door, the night owls are still waking up. They have black belts, so I would not want to come in loudly and ruffle their feathers! With all my excitement and happiness at having made it this far, one deep breath in and out grounds me for the adventurous hour ahead. I exhale gently and quietly bow, stating that I am ready to learn: "onegaishimasu."

Martial Art Love
Andrea Harkins

I can kick and punch to my heart's delight. I can yell and roar, if I want. After twenty plus years in the martial arts, I have learned a thing or two about the physical nature of martial arts. There is much more involved than going to the dojang, teaching, or writing about my experiences. The biggest thing I have learned from martial arts is not how to defend, fight, or battle, but how to love.

I naturally throw love into the mix because of my personality. Love is a trait that gives me a deeper perspective about what a martial art really means to me. For my younger students, I am a substitute mother who, depending on the situation, dries tears, offers praise, disciplines, and holds hands.

For adult women, I am a friend and someone who understands. I have been where they are. I know the cycles that weave in and out of their lives. I understand their desire to quench a thirst for learning.

Male martial artists consider me a martial art sister. We are equals, yet we play vastly different roles. Together, we create the big martial art picture. As brothers and sisters, we create the martial art family. These roles define my martial art sense of love.

I learn about love through my teacher-student relationships and my own personal growth. I want what I teach to translate into a memory for my students, so when they look back, they recall being inspired and encouraged through their martial arts experience. I want them to understand that martial arts taught them to live purposefully. This kind of martial art legacy evolves through love.

Recently, I received a beautiful handmade card from a boy in one of my classes. His grandmother has custody of him because his own parents had abandoned him. He lacked focus, with good reason. I often felt I was a little harsh on him, as I tried to get him to pay attention, or not touch other kids in class. I never realized the true impact that I made by being a consistent, but fair, instructor and disciplinarian.

He made the card because he was going to take the summer off from classes, and wanted to give me a present. On the cover of the handmade card, beneath the words, "Dear Mrs. Harkins," was his six-year-old version of the two of us, bowing to each other.

Inside, it said, "I love how nice you are. And I love it when you help me." When I read it, I sat quietly and cried. I thought to myself, this is it, this is why I do this. This is love, through martial arts.

This kind of love is not possible if you only focus on yourself. If you are selfish, it is unreachable and unattainable. Only when you have understanding and compassion for others, can you ever come to realize martial art love. When you want what is best for someone else, and do everything in your power to help others achieve, love naturally evolves.

Generally, there are two types of martial artists, although both have a sense of martial art love. Some have impeccable physical techniques. Their pure athleticism, flair, grace, and balance are obvious, and you cannot help your mouth from falling wide open when you witness their performances. I am amazed and in awe of their abilities, which clearly has taken several years of practice and a love for their art.

The other kind of martial artist is like me. I am not going to "wow" you with anything, but I am solid, secure, confident, and focused. I enjoy teaching and sharing, coaching and believing. The traits that make up my gifts and talents as a martial artist.

My role as a female martial artist is the conduit through which I can establish meaningful and loving martial art relationships. Love through martial arts has propelled me to where I am today, more than a martial artist and instructor, but a writer and motivator.

Although "love" may not be the first word that most practitioners use to describe martial arts, I think it is a necessary element in my practice. Martial arts are not just about facing battles and conflicts, defending, or fighting back. Martial art love creates an impact far greater than that.

.

THE FIGHTER

You measure the size of the accomplishment by the obstacles you had to overcome to reach your goals.
Booker T. Washington

The Joy of Fighting
Andrea Harkins

In 1973, Joy Turberville was touted the first and only woman to be rated in the top ten men's division as a fighter (Professional Karate Magazine, 1973). Often described as the toughest female fighter in the nation, her influence has helped other women today climb the ranks in MMA and other combat sports.

Joy's black belts are not in just one or two arts. She has rankings from 10th Dan to first Dan, in numerous martial arts, and her list of "firsts" in the martial arts is overwhelming.

Among them, she is the first woman to receive the rank of black belt in the Yuan Wha Ryu Karate system, (reference: Grand Master Man Hee Han), and currently holds a 5th Dan in this style. She was the first woman in the state of Texas to own and operate her own karate school, and the first, and possibly only woman, to achieve 5th Dan ranking in Song Moo Kwan Karate in the state of Texas.

Interestingly, she was also the first and only woman chosen by a group of approximately 30 Korean ROKS (Republic of Korea Marines) as a student (San Antonio, TX Brooks AFB).

These breakthroughs as a female martial artist and female fighter have earned her the label of a living legacy. It all started in Amarillo, Texas back in 1964, when she began training under the guidance of GM Tim Jo in Kodokan Judo. In 1965, she entered training in Moo Duk Kwan Tang Soo Do, with GM David Moon. Three years later, in 1968, she relocated to San Antonio, Texas.

There was a group of Korean ROKS in the area, and they watched her work out for about a month. After their intensive review, they advised her that they had chosen her as their one and only student for the duration of their stay in the USA.

In 1969, Joy moved to Dallas and trained in Shin Toshi with GM Mickey Fisher. In 1970, she trained in Parker's Chinese Kenpo with GM Larry Caster. In 1978, she began her training in Yuan Wha Ruy with GM Master Man Hee Han. In 1983, Joy opened USA KARATE.

Joy Turberville has held first place in national tournaments, such as the U.S. Championships, U.S. Tae Kwon Do Championships, USKA Nationals, All Style Open Nationals, and Karate Olympiks (A large tournament hosted by George Minshew, spelled with a "k"). These were just some of the tournaments in which she participated and won. Her skills were of championship quality, but it became difficult for her to use her competitive edge without disqualification.

While her background and history in the arts is impeccable, her fighting is what exemplified her true spirit. She stood out, not because she was a woman in the arts, but because she was good. She was so good, in fact, that at times she had to curtail her fighting. Either she was disqualified, or she won first place. She trained, taught, and fought with male world champions, and they influenced her greatly.

She had the opportunity to work with Grand Master Caster. His school name, Martial Arts Karate, implied that he taught more than just karate. Master Larry Caster was not only her friend and mentor, but he was also her trainer when she achieved the distinction of a fighter ranking. He also trained other legendary martial arts masters, such as "The Golden Greek", Demitrius Havanas, and Grand Master Roy Kurban.

It is difficult to imagine what these fight classes, hosted by Grand Master Caster, were like. Joy describes these Friday night fights as "brutal classes with as many as four individual matches occurring simultaneously." The classes were open and seriously challenged anyone who wanted to battle every major fighter in the Dallas Fort Worth Metroplex. Many others traveled from all over the U. S. to sharpen their game and learn new skills.

These open fight nights were often bloodbaths, with a minimum of one knockout per class. World champions from all weight classes fought bare knuckled, and without even a mouthpiece. Each fighter was ready, willing, and able to inflict maximum damage upon the other.

Martial artists such as Demetrius Havanas, Roy Kurban, Ray McCallum, Phil Wilemon, Benny Uriquidez, Joe Lewis, Mike Stone, Chuck Norris, and Ronnie Cox, steadily improved as fighters, while trying not "to slip down in the blood before it got mopped up," Joy shares.

This was the nature of Grand Master Caster's fight class, and a testimony to just how tough the fighters of that era were. This training allowed Joy to excel in competition, and earn a number ten ranking in the men's fighting division by *Professional Karate Magazine*.

Joy Turberville excelled in an era when female martial artists were scarce, and female fighters were not yet established. She learned from the best of the best and earned the coveted designation as a female fighter. Today, Joy Turberville continues to inspire and motivate others in martial arts.

While her training as a female powerhouse in a man's world is interesting, there is a lot more to the story that makes this woman truly remarkable. Her reason for learning a martial art and becoming a fighter are possibly different than you may think. She is, unmistakably, the Joy of fighting. Her candid and deeply personal journey is in the next chapter.

Against All Odds
Joy Turberville

I am frequently asked by interviewers the question, "When did you decide that you wanted to become a karate fighter, and what was your overall plan in the pursuit of that goal?"

I know that they are expecting a splendid tale of how I walked into a kickboxing class, saying to myself, "I can do this, and I can do it better than anyone else!" They think that I had a daily plan of how to attend and win every karate tournament.

The only problem with that fantasy scenario is that none of it is true. The idea of being in a place where people were striking each other or trying to beat each other up was abhorrent to me. I never wanted to be in that place. I had no desire or plan to win my way to the top of the national rankings, including number one in the top ten of the women's fighting division, but that is what happened.

I am going to tell you the truth. I came from a different time, when women were inferior, not capable of intellect, and very inept, especially in physical strength and athletic ability. There were no sporting events for girls at the schools I attended. Even if there had been, girls who were proper and dignified would not have participated because sports were unladylike.

Girls should never present any kind of a challenge to the male ego that is what I learned from the moment of my existence on this earth. Everyone believed that if a girl defeated a boy, it would only be through some unusual or bizarre accident. That despicable and unwarranted defeat would damage his ego, and it would inhibit him from being the superior being he was. A kinder act would be to maliciously put a bullet through his head and get his agony over with quickly and mercifully!

To put the matter bluntly, I never intended to achieve ranking in the top ten men's fighting division. At the time, I would not have been psychologically capable of thinking it, or wishing for it, because of the role women played during this time.

How did I become "The Legend," and ranked as one of the most skilled and powerful black belt fighters, either male or female, to land on the shores of the American karate landscape? It all started with David Moon.

When I first met David Moon, my first thought was, "Why is he frowning like that?" I noticed that his eyes and mouth were both turned down. His countenance was one of disdain and palpable distaste when he finally said, "She can come into the class, but she will not be treated as a woman. She will be trained with the same intensity as my other students, so be prepared for the fact that she probably will not last even one week in Moo Duk Kwan."

I could feel my face turn red and hot with embarrassment at the obvious fact that Mr. Moon, my husband Richard's karate teacher, had a very low opinion of women. He obviously did not want to disgrace his dojang by allowing the presence of one of these inferior creatures in his class. To complicate matters, I had absolutely no interest in learning a martial art of any kind.

I preferred spending my time in art museums and attending concerts performed by the Lubbock Symphony Orchestra. A recent visit by Van Cliburn thrilled me. My friend, Danny, had arranged the meeting as his birthday gift to me. Van Cliburn's polite and gracious treatment of me made a deep and lasting impression that I will never forget, because he made certain that I was treated with dignity and respect on my very special 24th birthday.

I also had the privilege of being a model for sculptor, Bess Hubbard, for the carving in stone of Madonna and Child. *Life Magazine* named Bess "Miss Art of West Texas," in a beautifully photographed spread in the magazine. Bess had just finished a bronze bust of my head which she simply named Joi (French for Joy), and it was immediately purchased and put on display in a museum somewhere on the east coast. These were my interests, and the kinds of things I loved doing.

The fact was that I did not want to be in a karate class, any more than David Moon wanted me there. I was polluting his class of male warriors! My mind raced frantically for a way out that would not actually amount to me breaking my word to my husband, but nothing brilliant came to mind.

I sat in the presence of two men, who were talking about me as if I were not even in the room. David reiterated that it was inconceivable that I would be able to endure even a week of his training. Somehow, the two men arrived at the conclusion that Dai Won Moon would allow me as his first female student, ever.

Richard and I had tried many new things together, and for the most part, I enjoyed the chess tournaments, the fencing classes, and being up in the air with him as pilot. Even the judo class had turned out to be fun, and I excelled under the excellent instruction of Tim Jo. He was a Chinese sensei who taught Kodokan judo, and explained everything with his one of a kind Texas accent.

As it turned out, I learned to love judo, but the idea of people hitting each other was an unbearable thought to me. Richard did an excellent job of selling the idea to me as something we could do together, and I had given my word that I would at least try it. In the back of my mind, I thought that Mr. Moon's brutal honesty was right. There was no way I would last.

Just a month before this whole introduction into karate, I was sitting quietly at my desk in Psychology 101 reading our current assignment. The hair on the back of my neck began to bristle as I read the section on human intelligence. The text contained a lengthy chapter on Darwin's theory that women were intellectually, morally, and physically inferior to the male. The male, he concluded were more highly evolved than the female. That was not the worst of it!

Darwin concluded that adult females, of most species, resembled the young of both sexes. From this and other evidence, he reasoned, "males are more evolutionarily advanced than females." Many contemporary anthropologists concluded, "Women's brains were analogous to those of animals," which had an "overdeveloped" sense organ "to the detriment of the brain" (Fee, 1979:418).

Carl Vogt, a University of Geneva natural history professor who accepted many of "the conclusions of England's great modern naturalist, Charles Darwin," argued that "the child, the female, and the senile white" all had the intellect and nature of the "grown up negro" (1863:192)".

My mind dissociated when I was thinking about this. I found myself back in the year that I had spent in West Point Mississippi as a teenager. As my sister, her husband, and I crossed the West Point city limits, I saw a huge billboard. It had an enlarged photograph of what appeared to be men on horseback with long crosses in their left hands. The men were wearing flowing, draped white uniform of sorts. They wore a kind of pointed white pyramidal shaped headdress, with eyes cut from the cloth so they could see, and a hole cut for the mouth.

The billboard said in shouting, huge, bold script, "The Klu Klux Klan of West Point Mississippi Welcomes You." I had never heard of the Klu Klux Klan, and I asked my brother-in-law who they were. I would rather not quote him, but his response made my soul shudder.

While in West Point, I worked as a waitress to earn gas money and to purchase new clothes. I made friends with the kitchen staff, which was difficult, because none of those sweet, hardworking people would look me in the eye. They all called me Miss Joy, even though I was years younger than they were.

I called them Ma'am and Sir, which they quickly asked me not to do. I found myself whispering to these new friends, to ask what was wrong. One woman in her 80's asked if she could come to work for me. She said she could do my ironing and washing, so I quickly hired her. I thought it would give us a chance to talk, and she could explain things to me once we were alone at my house. Her name was Eerie.

I learned that Eerie would work all day and all night if she had the opportunity. Many times, she was down on her knees scrubbing floors for people to earn enough money to purchase her grandchildren what they needed for school. To me, Eerie was the Mother Teresa type, although at the time, Mother Teresa was unknown to me.

I admired Eerie. I had never met anyone like her before. I thought she was the most beautiful person I had ever met. I helped her with all her work. I picked her up and took her home each day. I tried to talk to her while we were at work in the restaurant, but she always begged me not to do so.

I heard whispers around town that people were being hanged in trees. I received a phone call from the man who owned the restaurant where I worked. He said that he, the mayor and some of the council members wanted to have a meeting with me. They said it was best if I did not tell anyone else about it.

I was just a kid, and very naive. I showed up and sat at the table with some huge, angry looking men, not knowing why they had asked to meet with me. As it turned out, they were the top leadership of the local Klu Klux Klan. They told me that they had heard me referring to certain people as ma'am and sir, and that I had been telling them that it was all right for them to look me in the eye. I had been seen helping them do their work in the kitchen and, worst of all, I was seen driving them around town in my car.

The child inside of me spoke out, and I told these men that they had no right to treat anyone the way that they were treating my friends. I made it known that my friends deserved my respect, but that they did not.

The men looked as if they were going to explode (most of them were very toadish looking in the first place, and their red, angry looks were very unbecoming to their opulent faces). They began telling me all the reasons that I should despise the people around whom this discussion revolved, and what the results of my actions would be if I did not immediately change how I treated my friends.

I had no one to whom I could turn for advice, especially about something that I did not completely understand. I knew that my soul was screaming because what I was hearing was wrong, and I said so. I told the men that I had no desire to change any of my attitudes, and that nothing that they could say or do could change that!

They all stood up at the same time, put their hats on and left the restaurant in a huff. It looked a little like an old black and white movie from the 1940s. They were all stilted and huffy looking in their khaki pants and ecru colored hats.

The next week was full of phone calls of heavy breathing and telephone hang-ups, and then it happened. I was sitting down, eating the most delicious coconut pie that Eerie had ever made. She made it because she knew how much I liked it. It was break time at the restaurant, and I was relaxing and thinking of trying to get home in time to watch the Carol Burnett show.

I felt strong hands pick me up and turn me around in mid-air, and slung over someone's shoulder. I realized it was Butch, of all people, doing the man handling. Butch was the local high school football star quarterback, who was treated as a hero by everyone in West Point, especially all the men in town. He was a winner, and everyone treated him as if he was a little demigod.

I had gone to a drive-in movie with Butch the week before. He had a crush on me, and I made him take me home when he reached over and tried to hold hands with me. All my boyfriends always treated me with respect, and I was known as a good girl. As far as I was concerned, I did not care if he was the President. We only had one date, and it was much too early for all that hand holding stuff.

I had no idea what was happening, and everyone in the restaurant just went on eating as if this was commonplace. I was yelling at Butch and demanding that he put me down. Instead, he carried me out to his 57 Chevy, pushed me in from the driver's side, and took off.

I asked him if he had gone crazy, but he would not answer me. He just drove very fast. I could not get anything out of him. He stared straight ahead, and he finally turned down a little dirt road and drove for about a mile before finally stopping.

He reached over and grabbed me. He started to kiss me forcefully. I yelled at him and demanded to know what had possessed him. I told him that I knew him, and that I knew that he did not want to do this. I kept talking to him and finally he broke down and started crying.

He told me that he just could not go through with what they ordered him to do. It was then that I learned that they commanded him to abduct and rape me. This order had come from the men with whom I had spoken at the meeting. They told Butch that if he did not straighten me out, that they would, and no one would ever hear from me again.

We sat there, both sobbing and holding each other, as if we were a hurt little brother and sister who had just witnessed something so horrible as to defy description. After a while, he drove me home and neither of us talked. We did not say goodnight; I just went into my house, went into my bedroom and continued to cry. I could not fathom how those men could have that much hatred in their hearts, or how they could do the terrible things that they did to other human beings.

Everything that I had learned about hatred towards women and hatred towards people with skin that was a different color, I learned the hard way. I learned some monstrous things personally, instead of through the media, or by reading a good book on the subject.

I was shocked back into the present moment, when my psychology professor asked me if I would like to come with him and help do a microelectrode implant into a monkey's brain. Since I was still in another world and time when he spoke, it felt as if he were screaming from another dimension. It felt like a rapidly moving Ferrari, and I was jolted back into my seat in psychology class.

He asked me again, but I did not answer. Instead, I slammed the textbook with the lies down and walked out of class. I did not explain myself, and I never went back. I was hurt. I was steaming mad, but also hurt. I knew that I did not want to go through another attempt to be brainwashed into believing a horrible lie.

Why these stories are important in an understanding of my interaction with martial arts is that I had no idea that deep down inside I was already a warrior and a fighter. I knew that I had an affinity for the underdog, and that I always tried to take care of those around me who were experiencing bad things in their lives. I had never even seen a fight, and I was sure I did not want to.

I also knew that Tim Jo's judo class had changed me. I had experienced something that seemed odd in my judo classes. For the first time in my life, I interacted with men who encouraged me to compete with them, and they did not mind if I sometimes got the best of them in our competition.

They seemed proud of me. If I developed and understood a throw and could perform it better than them, their egos did not wilt at all. I had a sense of camaraderie for the first time in my life, and it fundamentally changed how my brain and mind functioned. It was all good!

There was still confusion for me in David Moon's class. The first two weeks were so difficult. None of the guys in his class would even look at me, and they seemed to resent the fact that I was there. David had come from the ancient styles of Korean martial arts that predated Tae Kwon Do, and he would tell us stories of the death fights that were common during the era of his instructors.

Moon had never seen a karate tournament before coming to America. He did not teach any emphasis on point style, karate competition. He always made us practice our kicking techniques with full power against rice paper, which we were required to touch but not tear.

Our uniforms had to snap with every technique, whether a kick, hand strike, or a block. In our one-step sparring, we had to kick or punch full power, touching the flesh without breaking the skin of our partner. Above everything else, he stressed power, form, and focus. His classes were 3 hours long, and Sunday was our only day off.

He placed our water cups so high on a shelf that we had to jump to get them to have a drink on our brief breaks. It was a while before I could jump high enough to reach the precious water, and there were many times when I would lose consciousness, due to utter exhaustion. When that happened, I would fall, and David would push me to the side of the room with his foot, so that I would not be in the way of the other students.

About 2 weeks into the training, David said that it was time for me to begin sparring. Admittedly, I was scared. Up until then, I had only watched the sparring, and it was brutal. I had convinced myself that he would exempt me from sparring, however nothing could have been further from the truth. David called up my sparring partner, a young man who had been a Shotokan brown belt, but was now a Moo Duk Kwan white belt.

He was an expert at kicking the shins with a blade side kick, and both my shins began to bleed. I could not think of any defense, since my only practice up to that point had been against thin air. I was thinking that David would stop the fight since I obviously could not defend myself properly, but he just stood there with a frown on his face.

Suddenly, something inside me changed. As the young man went for my bloody shins again, I hit him hard in the solar plexus with a David Moon style side kick. He shot back, as if he had just been blown out of cannon, only the wall stopped him, and then I hit his face with an overhand right.

David was shouting commands in Korean. I was so inexperienced that I did not know what the commands meant. I was continuing to execute kicks and punches against the now defenseless Shotokan stylist, until David and several students pulled me backwards out of the action.

I was so angry. I took off the white belt, threw it onto the floor, and said that I would never be back. As I was making my way to the front door David said "Turberville, pick up that belt. Don't you know that a Moo Duk Kwan belt should never touch the floor?"

For some inexplicable reason, I did exactly as he instructed. I turned, bowed to Mr. Moon, picked up the belt and finished the class. Once again, I felt a fundamental change deep inside my being. I knew for the first time in my life that it was acceptable to defend yourself against an aggressor, especially in the case of an aggressor being more powerful and skilled than you. I realized then that bullying was not ok, but defending yourself from a bully is the right thing to do, if you keep yourself under control.

Honestly, that night I was not in control, but from that day on, I always made certain that anger was not a part of my karate training. Within only minutes, I realized, to my surprise, that I had lost control. I also learned that I could mend that mistake, and never fight from anger ever again.

I remained in the class, week after week. David and I became fast and furious friends. He made kimchi and bulgolgi for me. We talked and talked. He explained warrior honor, student loyalty, self-control, and martial arts dignity to me. He spent time trying to explain his initial attitude towards me. He said that in his culture, women were on the same level as dogs.

He was the first Korean to tell me that women in Korea were required to walk several feet behind men, due to their disgusting inferiority. He said that I had earned his respect after seeing me never give up, and after seeing me train harder than any other student he had trained at that time. I found myself adoring him. It had been a clash of cultures, but reason and truth had won out. I loved him.

The first tournaments I attended were in small west Texas towns and in New Mexico. They were so small, in fact, that they did not have women's divisions. They forced me to fight in men's divisions to represent my school, and my instructor. I soon found out that the schools from more modern systems of karate and Tae Kwon Do obviously were not training as hard as David's school was, so the tournaments were fun, and our group would come home with carloads of trophies.

In 1968, Richard and I received the news that we were being transferred to Randolph AFB (Richard taught instrument flying to fighter jet pilots). At the very same time, David Moon received word from his superiors that he was relocating, too. David went to Mexico City, and Richard and I went to Universal City. I felt lost. I really did not want to practice martial arts anymore, but Richard found a Tang Soo Do school close to the base, and we continued our training.

One day, a group of Korean men in military uniforms came and watched the workout. They seemed to stare at me a lot, and I felt a little shy about performing in front of them. They came back night after night for a full month, when one of them stood up, bowed and asked to speak to me. I did not know what to expect. I thought he might address that I should not be allowed to train because I was a woman.

He introduced himself as Captain Song Hyung Kong of the Korean Marine Corps. He said that his group of ROKS had been looking for someone to train with while stationed in the U.S. He said that they had decided to choose me for training in several of the old Korean martial arts systems. I know the shock must have shown on my face, and I looked to Richard, not knowing how to respond to what seemed to be a scene out of a Hong Kong martial arts movie. I was speechless and never said a word.

Richard asked Kong where the training would take place. Kong said that we would be using one of the gymnasiums at Randolph AFB. Richard agreed to Kong's request if he could participate, too. From then on, we did our training with the ROKS, and I learned that Kong had formerly been the poet laureate of Korea.

Kong was one of the most beautiful spirits that I have ever met, in or out of martial arts. He would spend weeks at a time at our home. He did all the cooking while he was there. He taught me about Korean cuisine, the lost history of Korea, and the Japanese occupation of his land. He explained why he felt it was so important that he teach the old systems of Korean martial arts. He did not want them to forever die, or be lost, as the Korean language had once been.

He also described how prevalent and troubled the Korean attitude toward women was, and how it originated, despite of the fact that there were several famous and brilliant queens of Korea at one time. The ethos of a culture can change, sometimes due to only one pivotal event. During the reign of King Jinheung in sixth century Korea, a group of about 300 beautiful women called the Won Wa, were chosen and trained as formidable bodyguards of the king. Kong was animated and excited about explaining this to me.

These highly skilled martial artists were military spies and assassins assigned to take down rival nations and enemies of the government. They were especially famous for their skills with the Won Wa short sword. Two women oversaw what we would call today, Special Forces, the Won Wa. The women's names were Nammo and Cheunjeong. When King Jinheung fell in love with Nammo, rivalry and jealousy erupted between these two leaders and led to the murder of Nammo by Cheunjeong. This would change everything.

Upon hearing that they had recovered Nammo's body, the king went into a rage and had Cheunjeong beheaded and disbanded the Won Wa. The king posted an edict in every province saying that no longer would any woman receive any form of martial arts training, and that all women would walk behind men, alongside the dogs.

Women could no longer enter inside any kind of martial arts training facility, and they no longer held any of the revered governmental positions, which can be readily found in Korean history.

Before the invasion of Korea by Japan, the ancient Korean martial arts had a great influence on martial arts practice and philosophy. Even the Japanese martial arts adopted the war on women. Our American servicemen, who brought martial arts dojangs and dojos to the U.S., were influenced in their thinking towards women because of the murder of Nammo. Although they may not have learned the etiology of the attitudes, they still consciously reflected it in their training halls.

Song Hyung Kong explained that I was an exception to the rule, which had its roots in Korea's early shamanistic practices, and their belief in reincarnation. In Song Hyung Kong's mind, I was a special being. I did not argue the point with him, but I did not buy into the reincarnation theory, either.

By this time, I was having a lot of fun in karate practice. I learned that I had exceptional timing skills, and I absolutely lived for flying kicks. Every night I dreamed that I could fly, and I loved the dreams as much as the reality that I had exceptional jumping skills. After all, I had to jump for my water if I wanted any hydration during those 3-hour long classes of David Moon's!

Both David Moon and the Korean ROKS trained me to be a fierce fighter. I started to compete in tournaments, which had finally evolved into having a separate division for women competitors. The fact that I had trained very differently was glaringly apparent. I had to be so careful with my competitors. I could barely even touch them without it resulting in injury.

Women were not considered real martial artists, and were ridiculed, especially when it came to fighting. One well-known fight promoter, whose name I shall not reveal, told Shane Bondurant, an excellent fighter of the day, that he had added a women's division to his prestigious tournament for comedy relief!

The fact that ninety percent of the now famous black belt competitors and promoters looked down on us was hurtful to me, much in the same way that textbook in college attempted to indoctrinate me into thinking that all women, and all people of color, were intellectually on the same level as animals.

Although I was deeply disturbed by these ridiculous ramblings, I did not actively set out to right any wrongs. I very simply performed martial arts, and I was consumed by them. They had become my love, and I thought about them every minute of every waking hour. I dreamed of flying and flying sidekicks all night every night!

I can honestly say that I was never hurt while competing, but many of the people whom I fought were honest enough to tell me that they were intent on hurting me. Because I was small, I often competed with much larger opponents, because at that time there were no weight divisions for women.

I was a defensive fighter, and could usually counter offensive attacks with jump kicks. That was my favorite thing to do, because the timing had to be perfect. I had excessive power in my defensive kicks and my hand techniques, and often disqualified because of it.

I never followed any tournament circuit, and I was not the type of competitor who went to tournaments every weekend. I only went to tournaments that my friends talked me into attending, and I was just there for the fun of it.

I did not care about ratings or trophies, and would often give my trophies to children who were watching the competitions. The trophies were meaningless to me. What I learned about myself was that I enjoyed fighting with excellent male fighters, much more than I cared about fighting with other women in tournaments. I never fought women inside a dojang setting.

In several tournaments, nationally acclaimed women competitors would bow out, rather than get into the ring with me. My last tournament was The US Tae Kwon Do Championships, hosted by Demetrius Havanas. Advertisements touted it as having the largest ever women's division. Demetrius harangued me so much about supporting his tournament that I finally agreed to go. I arrived late, and the women's division was already lining up, and about to start. I had never seen such a large women's division before.

I noticed that two nationally ranked fighters dropped out and changed clothes when they saw me register for fighting. However, I was accustomed to that happening and there were plenty of competitors left. There was not a lot of time to warm up because I got there so late, so I asked my friend Nolan Johnson to do a quick fight warm up with me, as we often did, whether it was for him or for me.

Nolan was the best kung fu stylist that I had ever seen, and probably the best all-around athlete who has graced the earth. We were in too much of a hurry. He threw a beautiful jump side kick, and I countered with an obviously effective jump round house kick just to test my timing. The problem is that I accidentally knocked Nolan out with that jump round house kick. The entire women's division disbanded, refusing to risk fighting me.

Then I heard a rather loud discussion between Demetrius Havanas and the entire women's division. Grand Master Royce Young was standing right in the middle of the conversation, and he recounts that the Greek (Demetrius) was exclaiming that he had no intention of refunding any of the entry fees to cowards who would not face me in the ring. Royce tells this story a little more colorfully, but the bottom line is that one well-known karate instructor would not allow his fighter to bow out to me. I only had to fight one fight that day, and it only lasted a few seconds.

I never went back to another tournament after the U.S. Tae Kwon Do Championships. I grew weary of the controversy over the knockouts, and there was a movement by one group who tried to get me banned from women's competition altogether. It was just ceasing to hold any interest for me, so I chose instead to attend rather intense fight night competitions. I satisfied my lust to fight by restricting all my fighting to informal bouts with world champion fighters who were readying themselves for title bouts.

No one was more surprised than I was, when Professional Karate Magazine rated me in the top ten male fighters in the southwest circuit. I did not understand how the rating happened, because I did not follow any circuit and had no interest in being rated. It was only later that I learned that some of the greatest male fighters in the nation had voted for me. There was no women's fight ranking at that time, and they wanted me to be recognized.

Martial artists began calling me the "Living Legend" in 1973, and now I realize that the child who stood up to the Klu Klux Klan, and the woman who endured the terrible attitudes towards women martial artists, had seeds of greatness in the center of her being. She was a fighter who just did not know it, until getting into martial arts.

I overcame a lot for women everywhere, and especially those who followed my bulldozed path through the martial arts arena which truly occurred quite by accident. I think that you might be shocked to know that there is greatness inside of you, just waiting for the right circumstances for it to come racing out.

Speaking of greatness, now we honor awesome fighters like Ronda Rousey and Holly Holm for their elite fighting abilities. Getting recognition for women fighters has been a long and arduous journey. I like to think that I helped create a path with less negativity and a way for women to rip down artificial barriers. Just look at how far we have come and the journey just gets better and better all the time. I am a fighter!

What Sparring Taught Me about Life
Andrea Harkins

Years ago, I entered the sparring ring for the first time. I remember saying to myself, "Wow! These students are aggressive!" I was scared and frustrated, and had no idea how to defend myself against them. I could not pinpoint what I needed to do because I focused on the urgency of the moment and the fists and feet flying at me.

I lost that first sparring match and many others. The urgent thoughts in my head incapacitated me such that I could not focus or prioritize what I needed to do. The next fight was about the same, and the next few after that, too. I knew that I had to change something.

Finally, I decided to do something different. There was nothing to lose. I decided to take urgency out of the moment, to see if I could control my thoughts better. I told myself not rush, but to instead focus on technique and strategy. My mind had to process a new way of thinking. I decided to slow down, block, evade, circle around the ring, and look for the opponent's weak point.

I looked for moments when he dropped his guard during a kick, or if his side was open after a block or punch. I finally scored one single, solitary point. I had achieved my goal and identified a personal sparring strategy that worked for me. It originated with patience that created a strategy of timing, observing perseverance and never rushing the moment.

The quick pace of the initial fights felt so urgent, but that was not the right time to react. What mattered was slowing the pace, using opportunity in my favor, and removing the sense of urgency.

This lesson is applicable in life. If you feel like everything is urgent, sometimes slowing down is the better option. Do you have a list of incredibly urgent tasks, desires or demands that you place upon yourself or others? Learning to prioritize what is urgent in sparring takes practice and patience.

If everything feels like a battle and nothing is ever quite right, then you lose before you ever begin. Urgency is about perspective, and perspective is exaggerated. When you prioritize problems and challenges based on true importance, you erase the urgency and focus on what is important.

As I continued to spar, which admittedly was never my strong suit, I moved up in the ranks, and I got better at controlling urgency both in the ring, and in life. In tests, I often left with a "best performance" trophy, even though, athletically, there were much better sparring students than I did. The difference was that I learned to prioritize and control my urgent, but unimportant actions and thoughts, instead of allowing them to derail me.

As a woman, sparring for the first time so many years ago, I learned that no matter what your fears or inhibitions are, you must step into the sparring

ring with a unique strategy, and what feels right for you. Learn to appreciate your timing. Learn to sense what is important. Your priorities will change. Your unnecessary urgency will vanish. You will win.

Through this philosophy, you learn that sometimes losing is winning. It takes a loss or two to force you to figure out how to approach a situation the best way. Repeatedly you will make the same mistake, but one day, you will understand truth, and you will adapt by eliminating the incorrect perspective.

This is how to prioritize and change the way you think so you can overcome difficult challenges and obstacles. Trying to rush in the sparring ring, or in life, is not always the best solution. In fact, you may never get to where you want to go, if everything in your life seems urgent. Something must take precedence.

I always had a knack for looking for the opening. I seemed to be able to find the smallest opportunity to score a point because of my different perspective.

Sparring is a fascinating conglomeration of martial art defenses and fighting techniques. You should understand how and when to react. If you do not, you lose the match, and no one likes losing the match all the time. With these lessons developing within a short time with your opponent and a couple of judges scoring your actions, you eventually understand your weaknesses, and what to do to strengthen them.

When I examine what to do to score a point, or to overcome making the same mistake over and over, I realize that sparring taught me less about fighting and more about life.

Women of Wonder
Jill Diamond Chastain

My name is Jill Diamond. I am the co-Chair of the WBC Female Championship Committee. I founded the NABF Women's Division and World Boxing Cares. I am the ring finger in the first of a large sanctioning body, one that is trying to make a place in the arena for women boxers. I have been with them since the beginning of this journey in 2005. We are moving ahead, but slowly. In other countries, women are, at times, the Main Event, but here in the U.S. the lack of commitment from various promoters and Network executives impedes us.

I take women's boxing very seriously. More to the point, I take women athletes so seriously that I give up several hours a day, unpaid, to try to further their visibility and the philanthropy of our community.

Our snail's pace does not diminish the value of the ground we break. It has hallowed and built on the bones of the greats before us. What we do, all of us, is as important as anything else in sports, perhaps even more-so than another forty-yard goal or a three-point shot.

When I mention women's boxing some people respond, "Who wants to see women hitting women?" My response is, "Who wants to see men hitting men? "The point," I generally reply, "is to be so good you don't get hit."

It is not a brawl; it is a sport, or a type of complicated dance heard only by the two people in the ring. I am not here to defend boxing, but if you like boxing, you should also respect the women who participate as well. They are suffragettes in hand wraps.

It's a tragedy that today's women boxers may never be able to give up their day jobs, find suitable trainers, or make enough money from their winnings to cover their medical costs. Many of the people in charge of this sport are out of touch with its economic realities.

The television executives see women bouts as distractions. The matchmakers see women taking money from their purse. The promoters see a sure thing, only when it is 200 pounds stuffed in a groin protector.

I see the popularity of this sport resting on the muscled shoulders of these female athletes. Trying to convince the media is like trying to put a bowling ball in one side of your nose and pull it out the other end. Some are coming around, though. A highly-viewed victory of a former boxing champion over a renowned MMA fighter had two male boxers involving themselves in the publicity that came from the aftermath. These two boxing promoters have never promoted a woman's match.

Preachers must preach, dancers must dance, and boxers must box. It is a calling. It is too bad the shelf life is so short, and too bad the real head butts are from banging skulls against a glass tarpaulin. It is too bad the anxiety stems from finding a fight rather than participating in one.

That is the story, as I see it, and it is a story that is still evolving. Unfortunately, by the time it evolves, many of today's women may be too old to pose for the front of a Power Drink. I still believe it will happen one day. Ask Satchel Page, Poncho Villa, or Billy Jean King. Their bodies bled millionaires, athletes no better than they, who today are driving Cadillac's instead of taking the blue bus.

What about women's' boxing? I think its success is in the hands of twelve-year-old girls who will not be happy until they turn on the TV and see themselves in their role models. They are young amateurs who need us to keep punching down doors so someday they can stride through them, and in 2015, for the second time, the Olympics!

It is a lot to ask. They deal with the callous, disconnected sanctioning body; the promoters who make them sell tables, or the matchmaker who throws them in the ring with an unqualified newbie. Industry standards are lacking. We are all in the same business, but we are nobody's team.

These women fighters work out every day and twice on the weekends, after school, after work, when the babysitter arrives, in between casting calls, in between lovers, and in between hopes. They must. They pray to that they are recognized in gyms and youth centers all over the world, for who they are, what they do, with whom they train, and how far they have come.

It is not just about this moment. It is also about the future. One day those kids will be able to say that they learned footwork from their female heroes.

Meanwhile, women are living their dreams. They are filling out the talent pool and practicing the sweet science. They are doing the only thing they really want to do. They are heroes, trailblazers, and gatekeepers. They have the heart, the sweat, and the courage to be a champion. All that is lacking is the opportunity. Still, they win.

To Be Savage
Andrea Harkins

Female martial artists break barriers. That is why they find their martial art training exciting, compelling, and crucial. Prior to training, they were not equipped for self-defense or combat awareness. Martial arts and self-defense, although somewhat different, both provide essential tools for defense that can be life saving.

Training in a martial art creates self-assuredness. For example, breaking a board or sparring with another student in class, are both actions that require physical and mental strength that help a student feel empowered. Being empowered, however, is not enough. In real life situations, another level of defense must emerge, and that is how to be savage.

This sounds excessive or difficult, but along with trying to avoid or escape an attack, a woman must learn how to fight back in a violent manner, if warranted. It is difficult to think of a woman described this way. Think of a woman you love. It is strange to envision her as savage, yet, if someone were attacking her, would you not wish that she was savage enough to fight back to save her life?

Defense cannot afford to be calm, gentle, kind, or accommodating, if you want to survive. An escape from an attacker may require a fight that is fierce and violent. A woman may be required, at some point in her life, to be savage, if she is attacked, or thrust into a life-or-death situation. Every woman is capable of it.

In a sense, being called savage is a compliment when it comes to defense. It is about having the resolution, tools, abilities and resources to defeat danger. To defend those whom you love dearly, including yourself, requires an element of savage.

Being savage is not just physical. There is an effective strong mental component. I have read in the past about prisoners of war, abducted children, or others captured against their will. To survive, they had to focus on that which they could cling to in such desperate times. They focused on their relationships with family and loved ones. In a mental way, this was their savage defense. It was a way to battle the demons and the difficulties in their own minds.

What if you are caught in a situation where you feel something bad is about to happen? Do you ignore it? Do you turn the other way and hope for the best? I bet that there have been several situations where you dropped your guard and your awareness, and the thought of being savage, or fighting back, never entered your mind.

From my own personal experiences, I know that, on occasion, I have chosen to look the other way, even if I felt something bad could happen. If you avoid awareness, that is a dangerous reaction. You need to engage or activate your savage mindset. Make a mental decision to act instead of reacting.

Awareness is subtle. It can alert you to a potential violence or altercation. If you do not use it, you may find yourself in a compromising situation that requires you to use savage force, but, if aware, you may be able to avoid it altogether.

Prior to learning a martial art, I may have tried to strike out, scream, or bite someone's arm, if attacked, but I would not have the arsenal of savage defenses that I have now. Without proper training, I would have used a girly scream instead of a tribal yell. I would have tried to break free without any idea how, instead of using a trusted escape.

I am a stronger fighter and defender because of my martial art, and I can be savage if given no other choice. I want to know that I can save myself. I have no problem being savage, if it describes the fact that I will intensely fighting back for survival.

While I prefer to live my life peacefully, if I have no choice, I will allow myself to be savage.

Full Circle
Colleen Diemer

When I started martial arts, I was the only girl in class. I loved it because I felt protected, and it gave me a sense of family and belonging that I needed at the time. I was always athletic, and I loved challenging myself, so it was easy for me to rise quickly. I needed a place where I felt like I belonged, could learn to protect myself, and define my strengths and my power.

I learned about internal power, choosing wise instructors, and facing setbacks. I accepted surrender, toiled through broken bones, learned and taught. Through all of this, I have found out how to fight not just in the ring, but also in life.

When you think about martial arts, you assume they are about kicking and punching. It takes a lifetime to uncover the secrets of what is behind the history and traditions of why and when martial arts began. There is a whole world yet to discover. You can never learn it all. One part of it is the internal power.

Much of what I learned is about this understanding of internal power. Slow, meditative Tai chi forms are for healing and have some of the most amazing self-defense techniques. Some of the most advanced and powerful Kung Fu forms, such as the animal forms, heal different organs – the heart, lungs, liver, or kidney, through breathing and other exercises.

Internal systems, such as Tai Chi and Kung Fu, build your internal strength and energy, while healing your body at the same time. From the earth, the air, and the elements, power regenerates. Kung Fu combines these elements with how the animals developed and animals fight. Their fighting styles are so effective, and it is interesting how one animal can beat another.

Understanding internal power and strength is what helped me become a better fighter. I am a national champion with numerous state titles because of my mindset. Fighting is not just fighting. It takes time and effort. I wanted to look back on my life with no regrets.

At first, I thought that if I worked hard enough and accomplished all my goals and dreams, I would be happy, healthy, and everything would work out perfectly. Life does not work that way. If you dare to take enough risks, and if your goals and dreams are big and you go after them, you are probably going to end up making mistakes, too.

You will fail at times. You must learn to let go and learn from those mistakes. I accomplished most of my goals, but I had to figure out how to move around the obstacles that got in my way, to the finish line. Once I achieved my goals, I always reassessed and made new ones.

Some events in my life ambushed my goals without warning. In January 2000, after already earning three national titles and multiple state championships, my leg was broken in half.

This happened right in the beginning of the year, when it was time to start competing. It affected both my fighting career and other personal aspirations. I had started modeling and acting school at age 14. I began receiving good pay for a few years before my accident. The broken leg forced me to change my goals again, but I knew that if I worked hard enough, I could get back to them.

This injury took a toll. At the time, I thought it limited my chance of ever becoming as good a fighter as I should have been. Everything happens for a reason, and because of this setback, I began writing, which was a new and creative outlet for me. This experience reminded me that sometimes you should get everything you can from a dream, and then create a new one.

When I was asked to contribute for this book, I reflected on my life, my training, teaching, competitions, and fighting. I wondered what message I wanted to share. The biggest message is what martial arts taught me about life, fighting, and relationships.

When life gets difficult, sometimes you need to take a more powerful approach, such as yielding, or in a spiritual sense, surrendering. There are times when the more you fight or struggle, the more you will get hurt. At times, the mental strength to yield is more enduring than fighting back.

While training in New Jersey, we were working on a fighting drill. One person at a time would take turns fighting everyone else in the group. It was my turn, and I was the only girl. I was in the ring. After I fought a couple of rounds, each with one opponent, my Sensei invited two opponents to enter the ring at one time and fight me. Then he called two more in, and I had to fight four of them at one time. Then, he told them to take me down.

I had four large men on me, and there was absolutely nothing that I could do to escape or fight back. I was struggling and saying to myself, "What can I do, what can I do?" Physically, there was no defense.

They were not hurting me, but I knew that if this happened in a real-life situation, you must understand how to keep your mind calm. My Sensei often said, "When the going gets tough, the tough get mellow." Remembering that, I relaxed, and did not fight back. I had to rely on my mind, not my body, to help me.

This is a lesson for life and self-defense. If you find yourself in a situation where you cannot fight, you must stay calm and think. This is not something typically taught in every martial art school, but this training was real and focused on real life. It taught me that when a fight in life is too difficult, burdened with obstacles, or you are fighting too hard to reach a goal, let go.

Go with the flow and do not fight so hard. It was not easy to train this way, but it was about love, and about people who cared for me. They taught me to fight in martial arts, so I did not have to fight elsewhere.

Without these lessons and excellent instruction, I would never have become a champion. I consider every instructor with whom I have ever worked to be a blessing. Mostly, I trained privately. Each instructor has taught me valuable lessons through their experiences, teaching styles, fighting, championships, and business sense. With each, I developed a strong bond.

I always chose advanced instructors. I would go home every night feeling like a loser, but in a good way. I knew that if I stuck it out, I would adapt. I needed to be around the best and to set the bar as high as possible to become the best that I could be.

If you want to accomplish a goal, you must do the mental, physical and spiritual work. I had to stay focused, be committed 100%, and make sacrifices. I understood the value of someone trusting me. I eventually understood all the information they were providing. I was lucky to have the foresight and confidence to internalize it.

Black belts do not usually teach black belt techniques to beginners. At times, I was learning far beyond my level. I knew that I was capable of understanding and performing the advanced skills.

I had only one female instructor and fighting coach. She was a huge inspiration to me, and gave me something for which to strive. When I first saw her fight in the ring, she inspired me; I wanted to be like her. She showed me how much was possible.

There was little need to talk when I trained with her because there was an understanding. She probably already knew my story without me ever saying a word. She may have had similar experiences that brought her to the same place that I was. It was fun to work with a woman because her perspective was different from my other instructors.

I can appreciate where I am today, thanks to my training, fighting, my instructors, and the goals and aspirations I have achieved. I share what I have learned from my great instructors to my own students. I teach selectively because I know the value of what I have learned. The students I train make me very proud. They are pieces of me, and fighters with big hearts. They are survivors, and in a sense, they are my children.

I have also had the opportunity to work with people who have different types of disabilities and diseases. It is what I do best. Although I love seeing one of my students win a six-foot trophy, I also love watching others transform their minds, bodies, and spirits, through martial arts and meditation. It is miraculous, and a blessing to witness this power of the mind and spirit. I hope that I have made a difference for my students.

Even though I broke my leg years ago, I believe that I am a better fighter now than I have ever been. All the years of training without the pressure of competition helped me take the necessary rest and recovery that I needed to excel. Things that I did not realize were happening eventually revealed. After writing this, I realize that I should take nothing for granted. In fact, everything has a reason. The biggest truth I have discovered is that everything comes full circle.

There is no chance, no destiny, no fate, that can hinder or control the firm resolve of a determined soul.
Ella Wheeler Wilcox

Karate Born and Raised
Devorah Yoshiko Dometrich

I was born in the 1950's. I started Karate in 1965 at the age of 13. I was raised in the karate dojo, which was unheard of back then. In those days, there were a few dojos with many students, whereas nowadays there are many dojos with few students. Karate was starting to take off in the western world with the first generation of teachers. My adopted father, William Dometrich, was among them.

In the U.S., there was only one national karate championship. From 1963-1965, it was only open to men. In 1966, it opened to women for the first time. In May 1966, at the U.S. Armory, I fought 23 bouts, 2 minutes each, to become the First Woman's National Karate Champion in the history of United States, alongside Joe Lewis.

By today's standards, the competition in the 1960's and 1970's seems ancient. Forbidden was padding, hand and feet covers, and mouthpieces. The only thing allowed on the body was a cup that men wore.

A full punch was a half point, which illustrates how closely related it is to the current fad of cage fighting. Even cage fighters have some body protection. Each fighter squared off with the others, regardless of size, weight, or rank, which is unheard of in today's competitions.

Several years later, I entered the USAF. I received orders for Okinawa in 1974. It was the most memorable time of my life. They assigned me to the 376th SAC Wing, a service Wing to the SR 71, commonly known as the "Black Bird" or "Habu," in Okinawa. Habu translated is a poisonous snake.

I was the only female assigned to work in the Wing at that time and my fellow airmen teased me that I was too much of a tomboy to compete in the Miss Kadena Pageant. I told my supervisor that if he gave me the time off, I would win. I was determined. The Pageant lasted two weeks and I won the talent contest performing a kata, and I took first place along with Miss Congeniality.

I spent the following five years in Okinawa training in my teacher's dojo, Akamine Eisuke Sensei, the successor to Taira Shinken, founder of Ryu Kyu Kobudo Hozon Shinko Kai. Most GI's were white belts at the time. As a Ni Dan, I was fortunate to become his student, as he only taught Sho Dan and above. This adventure eventually became historical for several reasons.

First, I was the only person outside Japan and Okinawa to receive head of a country in Ryu Kyu Kobudo Hozon Shinko Kai when I was I was assigned as head of the United States, under Akamine Sensei. Next, in 1997, I became the first female in the history of Karate and Kobudo in Okinawa to receive a 7th Dan. This was only second to a 10th Dan in Kyu Do. Lastly, I became the only foreign deshi of Akamine Sensei in the world.

When I returned home in 1977, I entered law enforcement and was one of few women in the field. I spent the next four decades on patrol or teaching for the academy. Now in my off time, I travel and teach Kobudo to more than sixty dojos.

The endeavors throughout my life seemed to have been fate. One adventure after another gave me the confidence throughout life to get up and to move in a forward direction. Martial arts gave me the ability to know my limits early in life. I measured my limits not by gender, but by the physical, mental, and psychological ability to complete all my tasks.

TRAINING

A lot of times people look at the negative side of what they feel they can't do. I always look on the positive side of what I can do.
Chuck Norris

Breaking New Ground
Andrea Harkins

I have learned a lot about the evolving stereotypes of women in the martial arts through social media. Many share their blog stories, posts, pictures, and motivational excerpts, about martial arts. They have clear and concise opinions and are honest. Some are beginners, and some have been around a long time, but all of them have a story about how martial arts have guided them.

I am one of the female martial artists who shares personal insights on the web. I've noticed that many traditional stereotypes of the female martial artist have lifted, thanks, in part, to the new wave of fighting women, and in part to a culture striving for political correctness. Female martial artists are now respected because they have moved from one extreme to the other, from a time when they were not even allowed to practice martial arts.

I thought my female voice would only be recognized, or appreciated by other women. Men and women read many of the topics about which I write. I thought that men would read it and think that my personal application of martial arts to my life was a bit too philosophical.

To my surprise, many men readily accept and provide comments to what I say. Many aspire to apply more of these concepts to their own lives. This is a diverse change from what I have experienced in the past. Having been involved in martial arts for so long, I never expected that my martial art voice would be meaningful or encouraging to both genders.

Clearly, times have changed. When I began my training, women were still the absolute minority of practitioners, and their opinions were not as strong as their male counterparts were. Today, women finally have words of relevance, and they have listening ears, too.

They also have a stronger following of men than ever before, who recognize and respect their skills, techniques, knowledge, and mindset. When I ask men the question of who the better martial artist is, male or female, they are often quick to say women, for varying reasons.

In my mind, neither is better than the other, but it is refreshing to see the acknowledgement. Both genders are open and willing to explore the strengths of female martial artists. Men see the qualities of the female martial artists different from theirs, and perceive them at times, as better. Still, comparing the two is not the true test of the better martial artist, because they are as different as much as they are the same.

Strengths and talents are difficult to measure. Is it the belt, the degree, the physicality, or the mentality, that makes the better martial artist? Each gender seems to be exploring more about what the other gender already knows. In the current generation, women are pushing themselves physically as martial artists and fighters, and men are more conducive to mindfulness.

In my martial art classes for youth, there are a higher percentage of girls. Girls often become friends and enjoy working out together. When sparring, they have no preference if their opponent is a boy or girl. They enjoy the challenge either way. The stereotype that a boy would naturally be better than a girl in fighting does not exist.

In the adult class, the women are very devoted and committed, and their level of effort is exemplary. Many seem to have good self-confidence already, and they seek self-improvement when they walk in the door. If given the chance to break a board, most of them step up, because it helps destroy their personal demons. They break boards, personal barriers, and stereotypical perceptions, in one sweep.

Adult female martial artists who have recently started their practice have entered the martial art world at a time when women rival men as equal counterparts and are considered excellent contenders. For the older martial artists, like me, who have watched the evolution take place, the difference is noticeable and exciting.

I am not afraid to say that my experiences in the martial arts are uniquely female. I have my own reasons for practicing, and while I did not start because I wanted some type of empowerment, or to prove myself at all, that is exactly what happened.

By writing this book and having a voice, I am a spokesperson for the women who have practiced martial arts through generations of time. Because of my longevity in the arts, I am a part of the evolution of the female martial artist who is stepping out in courage and confidence while breaking new ground in the martial arts.

Falling Off the Martial Art Cliff
Andrea Harkins

Often, people ask me what it feels like to be a middle-aged female martial artist. This question makes me wonder why there are so few middle-aged martial art women, compared to middle aged martial art men. Why are people so impressed when they hear I am a black belt and an instructor at my age?

I had to break it down into pieces to figure it out. There are many middle-aged men who are black belts and instructors, who are very prevalent on social media. They are also school owners, experts, specialists, trainers, leaders, and are the main feature in every single martial art magazine. All these men started training long ago, but where are the women who started training with me back in the 1980's?

There is a logical flow in every martial art career. After you reach a certain level and attain a black belt or two, you rise to the next level of teaching, or you become a school owner. Like a parent, you hope to pass some of what you have learned to the next generation. It is a noble task and well needed.

The more middle-aged, wise people who teach the arts, the better the martial art world spins. They help raise the next generation with the traditions, nuances, and understanding of the physical and mental, and that is a heroic deed. Women, however, barely infiltrate any aspect of this martial art market.

While many started the same time as me, few continued. They did not have the chance to finish the loop from white to black and back again. There are exceptions to the rule, but there is no doubt that there is a deficiency of middle-aged women in the martial arts. Their paths were diverted, and they found themselves too busy, or too tired, to continue training.

How many female middle-aged martial artists are out there? It is difficult to speculate. Compared to the number of middle-aged men, I can conclude that the percentage is very small. They are a cherished group of older women, who are still active, teaching, or training. All the other women, over the years stopped climbing what I call, the martial art cliff.

Like climbing any cliff, it takes a great amount of energy, ambition, and resilience. In their twenties, women are adventurous, willing to take risks, and can spend free time as they please. They have flexibility in their schedules. As they become young adults, time is still in their favor. They have the time and energy to train and follow their passions. They are ambitious, strive to be good martial artists, learn, and advance. They easily journey to mid-cliff where the view is spectacular.

After this mid-cliff journey, however, things begin to change. Motherhood, careers, training, school, or relationships pull women in different directions. They only make it half way up the martial art cliff, before obstacles start to appear.

I do not think any woman thinks about discontinuing her training. Somehow, it just happens. With the next phase of her life, she finds it difficult to keep up with her martial art classes, because it becomes more difficult to find time for her training.

The momentum builds. If her significant other is not a martial artist, they start to feel disconnected when she is at the dojang training. Her children cry when she is gone. She begins to feel as if she needs more time to sustain her relationships at home. Soon, she pushes her "me time" to the side. It is understandable. Training wanes. Training stops. She never goes back. This is how women fall off the martial art cliff.

I was lucky. I did not fall. Throughout two pregnancies, I was completely active in martial arts. After the birth of my first son, I continued to teach. My husband and I took our baby with us when we taught at a community center for low-income families and high-risk youth.

I remember the employees of the center babysitting him, and rolling him around in a red wagon as we worked with the students in another room. As they passed by the door, he would cry because he wanted me, and I had to stop myself from running to his rescue, grabbing him in my arms and saying, "Okay, I'll be with you, instead of teaching the other children." I had to fight the urge to stop my martial art training and teaching to succumb to his wants, because if I did, I would dangle off the martial art cliff.

I felt sad to ignore him while teaching these students. I felt guilty that I was giving up my time with him, to help other kids. The tug of war was tiring and relentless. I continually asked myself if I should be spending time with these students who desperately needed me and needed to learn self-defense, or with my own child. I stayed.

I pushed motherhood aside for those couple of hours a week, to do what I knew had to be done. Teaching others while mothering my first son kept me climbing the martial art cliff. Little did I know that I was securing a place in my life, forever, as a martial artist.

When I was trudging through those self-doubts about not mothering for a few hours a week, I was basking in devotion and dedication to teaching. You cannot climb any cliff without believing that you are doing the right thing, and that you can make it. You cannot reach any magnificent height, unless it really means something to you. I had to overcome guilt by peppering it with my desire and belief that I could help others live better lives through the martial arts.

Babies two, three and four came along. It was crazy trying to practice a martial art and teach during those years. At one point, I did have to ignore my training for a while. I pushed it aside, but only physically. It remained in my heart, without a doubt. I knew that if I stopped completely, chances were that I would never go back. I would quickly fall off the cliff.

My male counterparts in their 30's and 40's continued their practice, because they did not have the same reasons to divert their training as me, or other women in my age group. My female friends started to fall off the cliff, one by one. They had too much going on. They began to embrace the skill of multi-tasking, but even so, they could only juggle so much.

To me, martial arts were never a commitment. Instead, they were a dedication. In later years, I watched some of the women try to return to their practice after so much time off. They forgot their training from years prior. They were like beginners again, and they were starting all over from the bottom of the cliff. I did not realize it at the time, but I was one of a few martial art women steadily climbing the cliff.

Other women are members of the lifelong club, too. They stand out because of their consecutive years of martial art practice. They are instructors, writers, and fighters. They are from the old school of thought, and still making a difference in martial arts. They climbed the cliff and never looked back.

For me, I sealed the deal and reached the top of the cliff when my family and I started our own martial art program. Commitment runs deep in a family who practices together.

I completely understand why the middle-aged martial art woman is a rarity. Because I kept learning, practicing, and training, I advanced up the cliff. It took the physical practice to help me figure out the mental perspective. That is why sticking with it all these years paid off.

I have been able to delve into the philosophical parts of my life more deeply through my practice. The wisdom that I have gained makes a difference. I help others find their potential.

This is my personal conjecture. I believe I have found the answer to my longevity in martial arts. It does not matter how many other women are like me. What is important is that I have secured a place as a life-long female martial artist.

Thankfully, I am still standing strongly at the top of the cliff. There is more to climb, if I so choose, but I am never going to look down. There is no harness keeping me safe and secure. I must be mindful to continue, to hold fast to this unique and special part of me, and never let it go. Standing proudly at the top has its own danger. If I can help it, I am never going to inch close enough to the edge, where I could fall off.

When you change the way you look at things, the things you look at change.
Wayne W. Dyer

It Only Took Thirty Years
Pam Darty

After spending nearly 40 years training and teaching Sukinaihiachi Shorin Ryu karate, I have finally made the trip to the roots of karate, Okinawa. It was the time of my life, and a very humbling experience, wrapped up in one.

After competing in tournaments since 1978, and bringing home more trophies than I cared to store, my husband, John, and I arrived in Naha City, Okinawa. We then made our way to the Budokan for kobudo training. In one day, I went from feeling like a winner to feeling like a white belt. It was not only an ego blow, but also a strain on my spirit.

My name was no longer Pam. It became, "Hey, hey, hey NO!" Long time members of Yogi Sensei's class told me that most guys walk out the first day because they cannot take the criticism. I saw the quality of the kata that was learned in the class; I knew that John and I were on the right track.

The most impressive student in class was a 60-year-old Shito ryu Master, Onaga Usuke, who looked like a 50-year-old martial art movie star. He was the All-Japan kumite champion 8 years in a row and is a "bad mo-fo," as they say. Even someone of this caliber defers to the deep knowledge of Hanshi 10th-degree karate Master, Jyosei Yogi.

I was almost 66 years of age, and had muscle-memory of only Shorin Ryu. It was difficult to learn so many different techniques, including stances, forward and lateral movements, hip engagement, and even how to hold the weapons. All of it was new to me. I wanted to put on a white belt and stand in the back of the class, but I looked around and saw only a few of us. I was the only woman there in the three months John and I attended the Budokan.

In the evenings, after training, the place where everyone went was the Dojo Bar and International Cafe. Every karateka who makes the journey to these roots should make their way to this martial arts-themed bar and café. Not as much drinking goes on, as martial art conversation. Historians, theorists, authors, sport karate folks, and traditionalists, enjoy socializing with others who have a martial art passion.

Everyone finds a spot on the walls to sign for their dojo at home, wherever that might be. All the bartenders and cooks are multi-lingual Okinawan young women with charming personalities. Most who make the journey are men, but I was fortunate to find a new best friend for life with one of the Okinawan women, Sunae. If you are in Okinawa, even if only for a day, you must visit this place.

I attended the World Karate Foundations Tournament on Thanksgiving weekend and saw several sport karate women perform fantastic kata. I overheard many of the masters saying, "No power." Most women who were sparring screamed so long and loud, it sounded like they were saying, "Oooow!" They continued even after they walked away from their opponent.

At the cultural events, I saw the strongest and perfect katas performed by young women in their 30's. These were not sport karate tournament performers, but traditionalists, who worked harder than their male counterparts did. These karate women, whose precise movements far outshined the hundreds of men around them, made me so proud.

If you have the dream, as I did for so long, of making the trip to the root of empty hand and weapons martial arts, make it. Promise yourself and save, so you can make the trip. Mix and mingle with the locals, even if you only know the polite phrases to say in Japanese. See the sights of the island and enjoy the people. You will never forget it, and you will never have the regret of doing the same old thing that everyone does.

No Excuses
Penny Pitassi

My very first studio was Bailey's Karate School in Rome, New York. The instructors were Vicki and Terry Donovan, a husband and wife team. When I started, I believe Vicki had just gotten her fifth Dan and had been a top rated national sport karate competitor.

This dojo was my first exposure to martial arts. Although I did not recognize it at the time, I had entered a unique teaching environment that had both male and female master level instructors.

This was back in 1990, when there were very few senior women in the martial arts. Because of that, I not only had a great role model for my martial arts training, but also had the opportunity to see how men and women approach their martial arts training differently.

I remember thinking, at age 19, how tough both were. Terry was a kickboxer, and he was big, rough, and tough. There was a picture of him in the entryway breaking a stack of five bricks with his head. I remember asking him one day, "How do you train for that?" He chuckled and said, "You don't train for that; you just do it." This turned out to be the nature of the school. They did not allow excuses. The training was difficult and the rank grading was even more difficult.

The great thing about this school was that the standards were the same for the women, as they were for the men. We ran wind sprints until you thought your lungs were going to burst. The women sparred against the men, and everybody went hard, even white and yellow belts.

I remember one specific time when I had to spar with Sensei Terry Donovan. He hit me in the midsection and knocked the wind out of me. It did not stop there. I tried to stop sparring so I could catch my breath, and he just kept hitting me and hitting me.

Then I heard his voice yelling at me, "You better not quit! If somebody on the street attacks you, they are not going to care if you are hurt or you cannot breathe. They are just going to keep attacking, so you better do something!" I fought back, because I had to. I was not going to get any mercy because I was a woman, or because I was hurting. No excuses allowed.

This theme ran throughout our training at the school. At my yellow belt test, I sparred with a man who knocked me down with a flying sidekick. I remember staring at him as he was flying through the air. I had never seen anything like that coming at me before.

He tried to do it a second time, and I knocked him on his butt with a side step, reverse punch. I dropped him right out of the air, and everyone cheered. There was no mercy for me when I landed on my rearend and none for him either when I returned the favor.

I remember another day when we were training on knife defenses. We started the class by breaking boards. The message was that there are circumstances in which you only get one chance to get it right. I was a 19-year-old yellow belt, who had to punch through a 12"x12" pine board. I hit the board incorrectly and broke the pinky knuckle on my right hand.

That was not the end of my training for the day. They did not dismiss me from class to go take care of my hand. I stayed and worked on the knife defenses with my other peers. At the end of the class, we had a mat chat about "toughening up" and about how in the big scheme of things, such as a car accident, or if we needed to run for help to save a family member or friend, broken fingers and toes or a little bit of pain were inconsequential.

To understand my circumstances, this training took place during my lunch hour at Griffins Air Force Base, where I was an aircraft maintenance crew chief on a B-52. When I went back to work, they looked at my hand and immediately sent me to base hospital.

I tried to explain to the doctor that I had been trying to break boards on my lunch break, as part of a knife self-defense class. I remember the doctor looking at me skeptically and asking, "So let me get this straight. You intentionally (emphasis on intentionally) hit something harder than your hand?" I replied, "Well, when you say it like that it sounds kind of stupid."

Then, I had to explain why I was practicing a martial art. He disapprovingly informed me that the Air Force considered martial arts to be a high-risk activity and required permission from my squadron commander. You could tell the doctor's attitude was one of "You're a woman and you shouldn't be doing this." He did not say it aloud, but the body language and tone were clear.

At the time, I did not think about martial arts as a man's world. I had grown up in the man's world. As a kid, my dad raced cars, and I hung around with all the people from the track. I helped in the garage during the week and went to the track on the weekends. When I graduated high school at age 17, I went straight into the Air Force with an assigned job as an aircraft mechanic. Again, I was in a man's world.

There were 400 of us working on the bomber flight line, and only two women in the whole group. We carried our own toolboxes, pushed heavy ground equipment and maintenance stands, and unmounted and remounted aircraft engine cowling. We did every bit of the work the men did, and most of the time we worked harder just to maintain our equality in the eyes of our male peers. As long as we carried our weight, they treated us the same, just like "one of the guys."

I did not understand why women were not supposed to be aircraft mechanics, or why women were not supposed to be martial artists. I was having fun, learning, and working out hard. The idea that something was more for men than women was not going to keep me out, especially when one of the head instructors was a woman. The cast on my broken hand kept me out of work, and out of karate, for several weeks.

I returned to training at Baileys after my hand healed. My first conversation with Vicki was my first indication that martial art training was perceived very differently by men and women. She told me that the classes were much easier now (1990) than they used to be in earlier years. The classes were formerly a minimum of 2 hours long, and the warmup was a 3-mile run. She said those who made it through the warmups and on to the martial arts training, were already strong and did not need martial arts.

She advocated for a long time for classes that transformed weak people into strong, and strong people into stronger. At that time, that kind of attitude was not prevalent in hard-core training schools, and not something for which the tough guys would have advocated.

This reality allowed their school to be more impactful for many people. If that format change had not happened, I probably would have never trained. Because of the training, I had at that school, I have been able to affect thousands of lives over the years, as an instructor myself. That ripple might never have happened had a woman's perspective, attitude, and inspiration not been present in that school.

One class affected the way I train and teach today. We were practicing scenario based training, and how to react if you are confronted by somebody in a bar. Many intoxicated people lose their inhibitions and become threatening, loud, and aggressive. We broke up into groups and had about five minutes to identify a solution for solving the problem.

They asked each group how they would handle it. All the male groups answered that they would try to create distance between themselves and the person or try to talk him down a little. In contrast, the women said they would palm strike the person in the face and knee him in the groin. The contrast was astounding to us, but our instructors expected it.

They went on to explain the disparity. Women are usually smaller and weaker than a potential attacker is. They also have potentially more to lose. Most men will see a scenario like that as a mild threat that might turn into a "bar fight," that is generally handled by de-escalation techniques. Because women can often be overpowered and must worry about scenarios like rape, they tend to escalate situations faster and more violently than men do.

A huge lightbulb went off in my head that day. Women and men not only perceive their training differently due to their size and strength, but also because of their mindset. They see the world differently, and so their training in martial arts is different as well. Everything learned on the training floor spills over into life.

As wives, mothers, teachers, and in all the other roles we fill, women need to understand their strengths and weaknesses. Martial arts training provides us with many opportunities to learn about ourselves and become so much more effective outside of the dojo.

It might appear as if I think my training at Bailey's was harsh. Quite to the contrary, I wish I had the opportunity to train there longer, but the Air Force had different plans for me, and moved me to Michigan. I trained there for less than a year, and they only promoted me two belt ranks.

It was an amazing opportunity that most people do not get to train under both a male and female master instructor, simultaneously. I saw how they viewed the world in a similar way, and how they viewed it differently. I think this provided me with a way of thinking about training that has influenced everything I have done in my martial arts and teaching ever since. My motto now is no excuses.

Blindsided
Janice Bishop

I never planned to become the first woman in North America to teach regular classes in Systema. I always loved martial arts and teaching, but I had never done either one for various reasons. Mostly, I was painfully shy.

It was not until I began training in martial arts when my mindset changed. The result was that a whole world of new possibilities that opened for me. None of this would have been possible without the complete support of my husband, Bernie, who unknowingly started me on this path.

In 1998, my husband saw an advertisement for a grading in a Russian martial art that was open to the public. We were new to Toronto and still exploring the area, so this was just another fun excursion for us. We had no idea that this experience would change our lives forever.

We found the gym in an industrial building, tucked away on a side street in Thornhill, just north of Toronto, Ontario, Canada. The grading was fun and exciting. "Defend yourself against two attackers while holding this cup of water and don't spill it," we were told.

There was a lot of laughter, and everyone seemed to be enjoying themselves. What captivated me was the feeling that I could do it. I had not attempted to kick over my head since I was six years old and I knocked the wind out of myself by slipping on my bedroom floor, trying to impress my older brother and sister.

This style did not use high kicks. The students also did not wear uniforms. Classes were not divided by skill level, either. They threw everyone into the deep end, and let them sink or swim – full contact, with no protective gear. At the time, I did not think about the lack of women in the class, I just knew I wanted to try it.

Apparently, I had a different upbringing than other people. Growing up, my chores were never divided into male or female roles. I did what I was told, and if I was told to bring in firewood, shovel snow in the winter, mow the lawn in the summer, do the dishes, and start supper, that is what I did.

Later, I learned from my father that there were female-only chores that my teenaged brother was not required to do, like washing dishes, but women had to do everything. I saw it as unfair, but the lesson I learned was that no one would stop me from doing anything.

Martial arts gave me strength and confidence. In the early days of my practice, I hid from the camera, so I was rarely in early video footage. I hated being filmed, even if I was just a bystander watching a demonstration. Systema demonstrations are full contact. Often the demos are at a slow speed, but the person on whom the demo is performed should be in good shape and have enough skill to avoid injury.

Stepping onto the mat for the first time was scary. Sistema is a combat style from the Russian military, and I worked a desk job by day, and had no martial arts experience. Just keeping up with the warm-up exercises was a challenge. I remember receiving a punch in the mouth for the first time. It was a slow drill, and I just watched his fist getting larger and larger and larger until it connected with my face!

I knew that they would not choose me for demonstrations because I was not ready. Then after a few months of training, the thought entered my head, "He might pick me." Total panic emerged. I started to hide behind other students so the instructor would not choose me for a demonstration. It was not fear of injury; I was afraid of being the center of attention with everyone watching me.

When I think back on it, I do not even remember the first time I was in a demonstration. Somehow, I went from hiding, to being in demos, to demonstrating on others, to teaching weekly classes. I even did demonstrations and big seminars in places like New York and Belgium. I know I would have never overcome that fear without martial arts.

I hope to inspire others through my story. I recently asked my mom if she would ever teach a line dancing class. Her immediate response was, "Oh, no!" When I asked, "Why not?" she said, "I would be too self-conscious." That is so sad, that an educated, professional woman who is long retired, still does not have the confidence to share something she enjoys doing with other people. What are you teaching the people in your life through your actions?

I never set out to be a role model for women. I got up one more time after being knocked down. My footwork was so bad when I started that I filmed my instructor's feet, drew a diagram of how he was moving, and practiced following it, to learn how to alleviate tripping over my own feet.

I asked one of my partners how he got so good at Systema. In typical Russian fashion, he replied, "You don't do your homework." He was correct. He did not give me an easy out. He gave me the simple, powerful truth that inferred I did not do well because I did not do enough work at home. It was not because I was a woman, or smaller in size.

That answer was very motivating because I realized that it meant that I would get better if I worked more. I did. I put in the time, took private lessons, traveled for seminars, and did as many classes as I could. Eventually I became an Instructor in Training, and then an Instructor.

Once I started co-teaching the kids' classes, however, I knew my actions and words were important as a role model for both boys and the girls. I learned a lot about kids. Guess what? Eight-year-old girls are quite capable of doing knuckle push-ups. They did not even question it. They just did what they saw me doing.

What had taken me years of pain and sweat to relearn, these kids were doing with relative ease because no one told them they could not do it. It is only later, through lack of physical activity, that girls stop being able to do full push-ups.

I do not think I really appreciated how big a deal it was being a female instructor in a military-based art, until recently. It was always my belief that if I worked to earn the respect of my partners and teachers, it would open the door for other women, by proving that I could do it. All I asked was to have the opportunity to learn.

I credit Jim King as my biggest motivator, coach, instructor, and cheerleader, because he treated me as an individual student and always pushed me just past my current level. Once I improved, I found other men willing to give me that opportunity and share their knowledge.

My biggest hurdle was that I did not understand the alpha male mentality. Once again, my husband came to the rescue. He explained that my experience alone was not enough, and that I had to prove I was better than new guys by physically beating them. Once I did that, things improved immensely. Eventually there seemed to be a tipping point. I cannot really explain why, but I assume that some of it had to do with the respect accorded to me by the experienced men in the art.

Eventually, after 10 years of serious training, I quit my day job to teach martial arts and fitness full time. Bernie and I were also operating a small bed and breakfast for Systema students from around the world. My social and work life finally merged into one. It was a great time, while it lasted.

I had been having trouble seeing faces clearly, but I just assumed my eyesight was changing, as I got older. One sunny Friday afternoon, as I was lying outside in my hammock reading a book, I closed my left eye and could not see the letters on the page. This blind spot in the center of my vision was the beginning of the end of my martial art career, just a couple of months after everything had come together in my life.

After a trip to my optometrist, the emergency department, three doctors and an emergency MRI, the diagnosis came back as glaucoma. Glaucoma is "the thief of sight," because it steals your vision with no warning signs. The disease kills the optic nerves that connect the eyes to the brain. High pressure inside the eyes can be controlled with drops or surgery, sometimes both, but there is no cure, and no reversing the damage once it is done.

Once glaucoma becomes advanced, the symptoms can include problems with contrast, adapting between light and darkness, and some loss of color vision. Anything that causes the pressure to increase in the eyes, such as tight clothing around the neck, inverted yoga poses, or playing a musical instrument like the trumpet, increases the danger of blindness. In my case with pigmentary glaucoma, this also included any jarring motions like running.

As more of the nerves die, there are gaps where no information reaches the brain. The brain simply fills in the missing information, which is why so many people lose a significant portion of their vision before being diagnosed. When I look at the blue sky, it seems perfectly normal. Looking at someone's face is a different story, however, since my brain's attempt to fill in the blanks with fuzzy, greyish color is not at all helpful. This can be challenging at times.

Still, I am one of the lucky ones. People rarely notice that I am visually impaired, until I use my white cane. For me, the cane is like an improvised weapon, just another tool to help me get through the day, no different than an umbrella that people use when and if it's necessary.

I use my cane in two situations, to avoid hurting other people when I am in crowds, and to avoid hurting myself in poorly lit areas. Although I generally try not to make a big deal of it, I am losing my vision at a steady pace. Every doctor's visit shows another 1-2% loss.

Am I concerned about sharing this with the world? Honestly, yes, because I am risking future job opportunities. I realize there are laws against discrimination in hiring practices. I also realize there are laws against assaulting people, and that does not always stop the assailant. I feel it is more important that people share their knowledge and experiences so that others can learn the truth, and not just accept current popular myths.

I have learned the hard way that glaucoma can happen at any age. Central vision can be affected, not just peripheral visual. The pictures of "glaucoma vision" is like looking through a black tube at whatever you see.

During one private group drill, one student was to hold my feet and another to hold each of my arms out to the side. The third student's job is to kick me in the stomach. He is a big man and easily outweighs me by 100 pounds. My job is to relax and absorb the strikes. Its purpose is not to toughen me up but to help me overcome fear.

The fear of going blind paralyzes me sometimes, but my martial arts training comes back and reminds me that it is just fear. I have overcome it in the past, and I will do it again. I remind myself to get up one more time, and to deal with the situation today and not worry about tomorrow.

Could I have stayed in Systema and continued to teach classes? Yes, but it would have meant not training, and not doing any of the warm-ups. I could not see myself as a person who sat outside the class, giving instructions but never participating. Some Systema friends stayed in touch, but most did not. I walked away from some. My career and my social life evaporated overnight.

I still applied the lessons I learned in martial arts, to make the best of a bad situation. I followed my doctor's orders, and kept to a strict schedule for my eight eye drops a day regimen. I tried Tai Chi. I changed my diet. I got a new desk job. I left that job and moved to a new province.

We went to Florida for two winters and made new friends who taught me watercolor painting, crochet, woodcarving, and wood burning. I practiced my

French. I even tried a few Systema classes with a favorite instructor in Florida, but every twitch and headache made me wonder if I was making myself go blind faster.

Five years after I stopped teaching and training, one of the few people who had kept in touch with me mentioned a woman named Olivia Overturf who was a Systema instructor in Texas. Olivia and I talked on Facebook and shared some videos. One of them was an old clip where two male instructors and I demonstrated a progression of how to build deep, heavy punches by punching each other. She sent me a video of one of her female instructors in Siberian Cossack Systema doing sword work.

At that moment, I did not know who was more excited. I had finally found that for which I had given up searching, a style in which I could train again. Her video brought back my initial, "I could do that!" feeling. Although we had never met in person, we had so many shared experiences. It was like finding a new sister you never knew existed. The Siberian Cossack Systema sword and whip work brought the spark back into my life.

Siberian Cossack Systema is not a military art, but a traditional art that includes women, children, and dancing along with fighting. Andrey Karimov, the head instructor, wanted women in his classes. For the first time in a very long time, I felt that I could bring and share my own strengths to others, even though I am physically restricted from doing some of the training.

Participating in my first seminar in five years, and meeting Olivia and Andrey in person, was the highlight of my year. I am so thrilled to be a part of this community and to be bringing Systema to Canada in 2016!

It never entered my thoughts that I would be a role model for disabled people. As I pick myself up one more time, I realize that maybe my experiences can help someone else. Maybe someone will check their eyesight instead of procrastinating, a doctor will be inspired to find a cure, or someone else will learn that they need to get up one more time to be successful with their dreams.

The idea is that flowing water never goes stale, so just keep on flowing.
Bruce Lee

Are Men Better Martial Artists Than Women Are?
Andrea Harkins

One of the most controversial questions in the martial arts is, are men or women better martial artists? There are a few obvious differences between male and female martial artists that I do not need to strategically point out, such as strength zones, body fat, and bone structures. Physically, their bodies are completely different, other than having the same kinds of limbs.

In some instances, men and women learn a martial art in the same way and have the same opportunities. Both can become physically stronger, more athletic, smarter, and more creative, through their practice. They are both capable of learning to defend, avoid harm's way, or face fears.

The differences emerge, and the similarities break apart, not in the examination of their physical practice, but in the mindset. Martial arts training provides a unique and conscientious empowerment for women.

Physically, men clearly have some good, natural advantages over women. They are stronger and more powerful. They have a larger bone structure, a denser body, heavier muscle mass, and physicality based on testosterone. Martial arts magnify these characteristics. When compared to women, their muscularity and body weight work to their advantage. Men have deep-seated instincts that control their competitive spirit and reactions.

I am always surprised when others want to assure me that men and women are the same in martial arts. To me, that is like comparing apples to oranges. They can only be comparable in intensity and focus, because when it comes to skills and technique, they learn and apply concepts differently.

Male and female martial artists are equally important and valuable, but never the same. You do not expect men and women in other roles such as husband and wife, brother and sister, or father and mother, to be the same, so why ever expect these two categories of people to be the same in the practice of a martial art?

With all this in mind, then, is the fact that men are stronger, larger, and more powerful, a clear argument that they are better martial artists than women are? I have the simplest answer to this question. Men are different, not better.

Thankfully, women have their own natural talents and abilities that contribute to their personal power, strength, and success in martial arts. They are intuitive. They are patient. They have strong hip strength and a high threshold for pain. Their bodies are smaller allowing for better flexibility and quickness. They have a strong mental clarity and a multitasking ability. These essential, innate qualities help in their martial art.

While a man can sometimes power his way through a skill or task, a woman must focus more specifically on technique. She generally cannot rely on brute strength or power to complete her martial arts tasks.

Bowling is a great example to show the difference between a man's strength, and a woman's finesse. I have seen a man powerfully throw a bowling ball and land a strike, even though the ball did not hit the center of the pins. They flew apart because of the force of his brute strength. A woman, on the other hand, must use a combination of finesse, skill, and technique to maneuver the same result.

The same can be true in self-defense. A man can overpower a woman solely on his size or strength, but a woman needs to use valid defense techniques to escape. This is the only way a man's size or strength can be manipulated and outdone.

A woman's mindset is also different from a man. Her intuition is like a sixth sense, or keen awareness, about what is going to happen next. She can sometimes predict an opening or a chance to score a point in a fight using her intuitive abilities. A woman's use of breath and her pain threshold are most noticeable in her childbearing years, and can be applied in kata, movement, kicks, throws, defenses, patterns, weapons, and her physical exploration of a martial art.

My first childbirth was completely out of the norm. I was advised that I would be in labor for hours, and how the whole processed worked, including administration of pain medicine. I felt confident throughout my pregnancy about what to expect when the big moment finally happened.

While at home one day in my 9th month, I started to feel contractions. I told my husband, "I think something is happening." Then, I joked with him and told him to eat breakfast since the doctor said it would take hours of labor.

As he was eating breakfast, my contractions intensified. We called the doctor and headed for the hospital. I was still assuming I would receive pain medication or an epidural, but the nurse told me I was too close to delivery, and it would be dangerous to administer medication at that time. I had to face the fact that I would have to endure it completely naturally. Nothing can prepare you for that. Let me repeat. Nothing!

The only relief was utilizing some of the meditative process and breathing that I had learned in martial arts. It was all I had, and I clung to it. The use of breath to endure pain was paramount in this situation. No man will ever understand, know, or share, the same use of breath or control of pain that accompanies the extraordinary delivery of life into the world. That is something that is exclusive to being a woman.

Beyond her boundaries of pain, a martial art woman has some other attributes that allow her to excel physically in her martial art. One of these attributes is quickness. Even I, a middle-ager, have a faster reaction than some men have.

The effectiveness of a technique is clearly the biggest advantage a woman can have in her martial art over her male peers. In my classes, some teen boys and adult men are twice my size. Even after all these years of training, I still question myself at times and wonder, if a man this big attacked me, could I win?

When a student quickly releases his grip based on the technique I have performed, I am energized and renewed. We both realized and acknowledged that my female strengths, combined with training and skill, worked. Against an untrained man, no matter his size, I have the advantage.

The discussion of who is better depends on your perspective. The innate power and strength that defines masculinity versus the natural attributes of a woman are on different ends of the spectrum. Can both fight back, learn the same skills, train intensely, and master a martial art? The answer to all is, yes. Are men better at martial arts than women are? The answer is, no. They are different.

I am glad to have different talents and strengths when it comes to martial arts. I never want to compete against their manliness. I would rather compete on my own merits, as a female martial artist. Together, male and female martial artists create the wonderful spectrum of martial arts. It is not a competition, because both men and women win, and both are equally important.

Martial arts are not gender specific, yet they promise different learning opportunities and applications for men and women. Both genders can use martial arts to grow, learn, expand, practice, and compete. In all fairness, martial arts help everyone become the best that they can be.

He taught him the secret to karate lies in the mind and heart. Not in the hands.
The Karate Kid

COURAGE

The most effective way to do it, is to do it.
Amelia Earhart

Growing in Courage

Andrea Harkins

Many years ago, I had a moment of martial art courage during my green belt exam. It is a simple example of how something unexpected exposes your lack of self-confidence and forces you to examine it. For the first time in my life, I had to summon courage that had been dormant for a long time, and surprisingly, I succeeded.

I was nervous all day about my green belt test, but when I arrived, I was focused, prepared, and knew what to expect. I thoroughly studied all the possible scenarios that could happen, and what I needed to do.

Everything felt right during the test. I escaped from grabs with ease, and my well-practiced routines were crisp. As the test ended, I was relieved and had a great feeling of accomplishing something good in my life.

That is when it happened. Sensei unexpectedly called out my name, and I had to run to him at the center of the floor. I had no idea what he wanted. This was not something for which I prepared. He walked toward me with a board in his hand. I had never broken a board before. I was petrified. Lack of confidence rushed over me like a waterfall.

Then, I noticed something else. He was holding two one-inch boards, back to back. My heart sank. My first thought was, I could not do this, as he declared to the audience that I would perform a jump front kick to break the boards.

I did what he asked of me. I put my guard up, jumped high, kicked and yelled. Nothing happened, except that my foot bounced off the board, and a quiet hush from the audience engulfed me. Try number two. The same thing happened.

By now, I was starting to feel a sense of dread and panic. I had to encourage myself from within. "He would not ask you to do this if he didn't think you could," I told myself. "All these people are watching. They are holding their breath for you. You can do it," I whispered.

Once I told myself, I could do it, my courage finally clicked. It was a turning point. I realized in a moment, that it is not enough to be told what to do. You must believe in yourself. You must tell yourself that you can do it. The third kick worked. I am sure the look of relief on my face was priceless. I almost did not believe it myself. Sensei held up two broken boards with a smile, and I was drunk with relief.

Nothing prepared me for this challenge and I did not expect it. The truth is it made me a stronger, more confident person in many ways. I learned that I must face challenges along the way to rise to my potential. In my green belt board break, I discovered many truths about myself as a woman. I was quickly reminded that I was not being all that I could be, or embracing all that my training had to offer.

At times, I still limit myself based on my gender, question my own abilities, or forget that I am capable of being as powerful as I choose to be. The true challenge then, is not what I am doing, but what I am not doing.

I cannot tell anyone how to solve problems or deal with the unexpected. What I can share is that you must examine your actions, goals, and beliefs, to make the right decisions in your life. A challenge requires you to give effort to succeed

It does not take a superhero or a martial artist to conquer a challenge. Once you conquer small obstacles, you will be more prepared to win when called to life's bigger battles. My growth in courage is just a precursor to life's more difficult challenges, and how I, as a martial art woman, can overcome, no matter how many times I try.

No Longer Bullied
Lynda Niemczak Hatch

I was born with a profound hearing loss, which no one discovered until I was 6 months old, when my parents took me to a pediatrician. I am the only one in my family who has this invisible physical disability.

My parents loved me and made sure I received the proper education. At two and a half years old, I attended special education for hearing-impaired. Later I went on to elementary school, then high school. After four years of college, I earned a Bachelor of Science degree in Computer Sciences.

I started practicing karate after graduation from high school at age 17. I was in my first semester of college at the Henry Ford Community College in Dearborn, MI. This is where I also met my husband, Dave Hatch, in September of 1969. After attending the community college, I attended Detroit College of Business, for another two and a half years.

Karate classes were held weekly at the community college. At that time, Dave was an assistant instructor in the art of Japanese Shito-ryu. I continued for the next two years, and enrolled in the karate club called Karate/Judo Schools of America a year later. My parents trusted in me to forge ahead in this art, and they invested their hard-earned money so I could pursue it.

About two years after my college graduation, and my marriage to Dave, I attained my black belt in the early 1970's. When testing for the black belt, I had to spar late at night, around 11:00 p.m., against five black belt males, including Sensei Dave.

I was tired and nervous after working long hours at my day job. The test involved six rounds, with 30 seconds of continuous fighting and blocking, and 30 seconds of rest, plus katas. The sparring seemed longer than 30 seconds, and the resting seemed a lot shorter. I gave my all, and I passed with flying colors.

At that time, I was the only female to earn this ranking before the Karate/Judo Schools closed in 1978 or 1979. Between 1977 and 1985, Dave and I still practiced and sparred on and off with different people in four Karate/Judo of America locations in the Metro Detroit area. A friend of Dave's from work mentioned that Dan Inosanto was coming to town for a weekend seminar at the campus of Michigan State University.

At that time, we thought it was too far to drive. Little did we know that we would later travel much further than that for our training. We went to the seminar with Dave's friend, and we were excited to have what we thought would be our only opportunity to meet Dan Inosanto, Bruce Lee's top student.

Dave and I were fully prepared to see him act aloof, cocky, or tough, with an attitude of a know-it-all, when we approached him. I was nervous and apprehensive because in magazine pictures, he always appeared mean and never smiled.

After being introduced, I changed my initial impression. His gentle and kind demeanor and his rare smile blew me away. I immediately felt relaxed, knowing this man was above board. His mannerisms squashed my initial consternation of meeting him. Dave and I enjoyed our very first seminar with Dan Inosanto, along with Larry Hartsell, and Chris Kent. It lasted 8 hours each day, and we were overwhelmed and burned out, but we totally loved everything we had seen and experienced.

I enjoyed the variety of motions and flows of Kali sticks and knives, Silat, and JKD trapping. In my eyes, it was completely different and exciting. The sponsors for the weekend seminar were Dan Timlin and Tammy Williams. After that, they taught us some basics in Kali, Silat, and JKD in a couple of private sessions.

This seminar in March of 1985 was another major turning point in my long and challenging journey in expanding my horizon by learning new arts. When I first began attending seminars and camps with Guro Inosanto, and during Dave's candidacy and apprenticeship, I never dreamed of being part of the Inosanto Instructor program, but that is what happened.

It was a long way from my younger years. During my elementary school years, I was bullied by a couple of hearing-impaired students at a cafeteria and on a school bus. I was picked on because I was the only one with red hair and had a different religion than most of the others. I also had better grades, and they felt inferior about that.

During those turbulent school years of my childhood, my parents were very loving and supportive of me. For quite a while, they were unaware of my difficulties. I was afraid to tell them, or my special education teacher, because the bullies threatened to attack my parents if I snitched on them.

Soon after my parents found out, they dealt with the bullies. I managed to get through these tough times with high grades. As I got older, and began my junior and senior high school years, I did not have these issues anymore. Mentally, though, I was still concerned that someone would bully me, attack me, or harm my parents.

When I was twelve, I saw a karate school on the other side of town and asked my parents about joining. They had to say no because they only had one car, and my father had a second job. I never forgot about the school, and it was about five years later when I eventually enrolled in the community college karate program that met once per week. That was how my martial arts life started.

Because others bullied me, I always wanted to learn karate to help protect myself. I could avoid places and situations that could put me in harm's way. When I joined the karate club in junior college, Dave became my ears, and helped me understand what was going on in the hearing world. Together, we continued, and still do, our lifelong training in many martial arts.

The most significant way that I apply martial arts to my life is through self-discipline. The greatest value of life is when you take control of your attitude and physical actions. You learn to set goals and research ways to accomplish them. I have learned that self-discipline is the key to developing self-esteem and empowerment. When I take the positive approach in martial arts, it helps in developing my philosophy in life and in setting my priorities.

In the art of Wing Chun Kung-Fu trapping, when anyone produces an obstruction or barrier, you remove it, and continue to move forward. One of my instructors, Sifu Francis Fong, always told us that you should use your mind to focus your thoughts on removing that obstacle. If you think you cannot, you will have the tendency to quit, stop, or retreat.

If you have a positive attitude and fortitude, along with applying the attributes of sensitivity to your life, you will learn that you have several options to remove any barrier. You can avoid an attack by slapping, pulling, or jerking the barrier, or just sliding over or under it to attack. This philosophy of training helps when training with men who are, in most cases, physically bigger and stronger.

Most men have the tendency to muscle their way when training. My Si Gung (grandfather) in martial arts, the late Bruce Lee, talked about being like water. Water adapts to its surroundings. It can be soft, and it can build up enough pressure to crash through barriers. Initially, water always seeks the path of least resistance when there is an obstruction. Another one of my instructors, Guro Dan Inosanto also guided us using this philosophy and it has served me well.

Another saying that I like is, "If you fight fire with fire, you end up with ashes." If you use force against force, head on with a stronger person, you lose. Force works best when you use it on the weakest part of another's physical structure. I may have to adjust my angle of attack to get to my opponent's weakest point, but it is better than being suppressed physically and mentally. The same applies to daily life.

I have learned a lot from a successful businessman, the late Jim Rohn, who taught that philosophy is what you know. It is a collection of your knowledge through observation, reading, and your experiences. Your mind is very powerful. There is tremendous potential in what you can learn and do. I have found that patience is a very important attribute needed to learn. If you are a student and always searching, you gather the information needed to accomplish the values of life.

As a hearing-impaired woman, I am only limited by what I cannot hear. My husband tells me that he sometimes learns things just by overhearing people talking to one another. I do not have that luxury. Because of this disability, I depend highly on visual stimulation.

I watch how things are done. Reading not just words, but also body language is extremely valuable for me. I read lips but this is not easy because everybody moves their lips differently. In addition, I watch what they do. I am sure all of us have experienced people who say or write one thing and do something different.

More and more women are practicing martial arts now as compared to when I started. When I recently received my Ajarn (Master) level in Thai Boxing (Muay Thai) from Ajarn Surachai Sirisute, there were around 140 people at the Oregon training camp. More than 50 of them were women. This is a far cry from the early years when I attended seminars. I gave a short speech (with my husband interpreting) inspiring these women to feel empowered and reminding them that they can do it. I encouraged them not to give up. There are more women in the film industry doing stunt work and choreography fight scenes now, too.

All women should keep a positive frame of mind about their potential. Martial arts are great for building and nurturing self-esteem and self-confidence. It does not mean that you can go out and beat up men! It means that you can develop the proper mindset to overcome adversity.

Julie and Her Hurdle
Karen Eden Herdman

Unless you are very popular, or athletic, I am convinced that there cannot be a more God-forsaken experience on the planet than 7th grade P.E. Who could forget being picked for teams by the "team captains?" It is a good thing that this seventh grader, who never was picked on, grew up to become a karate master. I wonder how any of us geeks made it through those horrific times in our lives. Evidentially, I did muddle through it all okay.

Even when it came time to participate in track and field, I remember being scared to death of having to jump hurdles. For some reason, I just went for it, and it seems my body knew exactly how to clear them. Hurdles were no more than an optical illusion, and I learned that very quickly. However, I will never forget a classmate named Julie.

Like me, Julie was a major geek. Not only was she unpopular, she was also way behind in physical development. Julie was small compared to the average seventh grader. Looking back, those hurdles must have seemed like a building for her to jump over. They came up to about the waist of an average 7th grade girl. Poor Julie. That hurdle pretty much came right up to her neck. She just could not do it.

Finally, at the end of one class, the teacher set up a hurdle and told Julie that the class could not leave until she jumped it (and yes, I do think that my 7th grade gym teacher was a messenger from Hell). Back and forth this little seventh grader went. I could feel her heart racing as she took off running, only to stop within a couple of inches of jumping the hurdle. The peer pressure mounted, and a jeering mob began to form as the class bell rang for gym to be over.

"My God Julie, just do it!" the other girls would yell. Julie seemed like a caged zoo animal. Back and forth, she continued to go, always just stopping short of jumping that hurdle.

Now here I am. Decades have passed since the 7th grade, and I often wonder about why a hurdle can seem so easy for the mass majority to get over, yet so difficult for any one individual. Julie's hurdle was an actual hurdle.

My hurdles have been many intangible issues since 7th grade P.E. I could today, in a heartbeat, set up cylinder blocks and bust right through them. Things that others have cleared so easily in their lives, I have often found scary and overwhelming.

I was talking with one of my black belt instructors about how we all end up with our own hurdles that we must jump over, and why they seem so scary to us, but not necessarily to others. "We are all merely a product of what we have experienced," I told him.

I am convinced that what happened in the first 12 years or so of our lives, equipped us to get over hurdles for the rest of our lives. Too bad my 7th grade gym teacher was not thinking about that at the time. Knowing what I know now, if only I could rewind the tape and just have a couple of minutes with this little girl. "Look, Julie, I know that that hurdle looks big and scary, but it's just an optical illusion. You can do this!" I would tell her.

The truth is I wish I could rewind the tape on my own life, and tell myself the same thing about all the scary hurdles in my own life. There was nothing I could not get through. It is the same lesson we teach with our big scary wood boards in karate. It is an illusion. You can break that board.

As for Julie, she ended up getting so worked up that she ran right through that hurdle and broke it in half, which to me was even more impressive. Kudos to Julie wherever she may be. May she get through every hurdle in her own life, no matter how she must do it.

The Journey Became the Destination
Marci Faustini

I am Sensei Marci Stracka Faustini of the living Hope Dojo, in Sturgeon Bay, Wisconsin, Dojo, number 7, under Soul~ki Peter Flores Duro y Suave. Thank you to My Hanshi, Kevin McGrath (who I am a Representative for in USA Goju) and Shihan Mark Stephens, and My Family of Duro y Suave, and so many more for guiding, teaching and sharing on this path of life. My style of Karate is USA Goju Ryu (soft and hard). For me, the journey became the destination and has become my life.

Let us start at the beginning. I grew up in Rockford Illinois I always wanted to learn a martial art, but because I came from a large family, it was not affordable. I was fortunate to have two male practitioners in my neighborhood who attended a local martial arts school. One of them was a black belt, so he started training me, with no mercy.

It was a daily practice in the outdoor dojo. Because I am dyslexic, others bullied and teased me a lot in my younger years. I quickly learned how to defend myself mentally and physically, and others eventually saw that I would not allow myself to be a victim. I slowly earned respect from other peers. I broke up many fights and got in a few myself.

Years later, an abusive boyfriend attacked me by riding his snowmobile up and over the back of my snowmobile. I used my training, and did not panic. I stayed calm, and ducked and rolled off my moving snowmobile. Wearing full gear, I ran and climbed a tree. As he rode up the hill to the tree and shut his sled off, I told him in a deep, quiet, but stern voice, that I was going to climb down the tree and get on my sled. I clearly conveyed that I would not deal with any of his macho attitude and that he was not to follow.

It worked! I made it to safety and called the police. I tell my students that you will always have time to break down after the battle. Since 75% of my students are women from the ages of 13-63, this applies greatly.

As we all know, men and women are wired differently. Men often act on their feelings, while women focus on their mind and spirit. There are many acts of self-defense, self-respect, self-reliance, and self-worth that take place. Autonomy implies that you can make decisions for yourself, and take responsibility for your health and well-being through empowerment, confidence, focus, and courage. You can learn to use your life training intelligently and without doubts or feelings.

Just as in Karate Do, you just do. You must be aware of everything around you, not trust others for your safety, and stay away from places that may put you in danger (example at a bar or party where someone can drug your drink). There are many self-defense techniques in martial arts that can help you avoid being a victim. It is not just about kicking, punching and katas.

Along with just "doing," I learned a lot about Chi (breathing techniques), which have helped me tremendously, especially after losing both my parents within two months of each other. First, I watched my Dad pass, and I gave him permission to leave, peacefully and with a sense of strength. Then, I found my mother dead in her chair. I had to use breathing (Chi) to stay strong, while waiting for the coroner and police, and answering all their questions until they took her body away. If not for Goju becoming a way of life, I would have been a puddle on the floor.

Another example of how my martial arts gave me the power to overcome difficulties happened in September 2014. I was out on a horse two miles from home, when my horse started to buck. I decided to dismount and when I did, the horse bumped me, and I started to fall, so I turned it into a roll.

The horse was still jumping and bucking, so I covered my head and rolled again. My horse came back around and kicked me in the lower back. I rolled again this time into safety. I laid there for a bit, then got up and walked two miles home through fields, up and down hills, and through a stream. What got me home was Karate Do.

I then had my husband take me to the emergency room, where I learned that I had broken my spine right above the tailbone. I never missed teaching a class and never stopped my training. I worked around my limitations and learned from them. There is no "I can't" in Karate Do. It is my way of life.

I often pray that I can continue. I seek the wisdom to pass my knowledge on to others. I hope for the power to succeed. My husband and daughter also train with me. It is a family affair. Through my training, I have come to know a couple of very important truths. The first is that our family is strongly bonded, due to martial arts. The family, who spars together, stays together. The other important truth that I have learned, thanks to my martial art training, is that whatever happens, I can overcome.

6'7'' in Heels

Karen Eden Herdman

When I first met Kathy, an acting coach, I could not help but look up to her, literally. Kathy is 6'4'' tall. I brought her in to work with my kids so they could learn how to carry themselves with confidence and self-esteem, especially the girls.

"I know you're saying 'Wow! She's really tall.' And that's okay," Kathy said to them. "Not only am I tall, but I like to wear high-heeled shoes. Why should I not enjoy a nice high-heeled shoe just because I am tall? If somebody's got a problem with that, it is their problem, not mine!" she went on to say.

I thought this was great. Often, women over 5'9" will usually resort to wearing flat shoes their entire adult life. I never looked at it this way, probably because I am not overtly tall, but a woman wearing high- heels when she is already 6'4" is a confident woman!

When I was a "just off the street" white belt, I remember seeing a master-ranked black belt vacuuming the floor at our federation headquarters. "I don't understand," I said to myself. The world would have you believe that rank and status will always demand that somebody else do the clean-up detail. Yet, here was this high-ranked master toiling with such an unimportant duty.

It would be years before I would mature into that very same belt, and then realize that performing such unimportant duties is because of one's strong sense of self-worth, not the lack of it.

Over the years, I have tried to contact various radio and TV personalities with whom I once worked, who were released from their contracts. The majority of the time, they never returned my phone calls, because they felt like they were somehow lesser of a person for being laid off.

"How do you maintain your dignity and face all those people who used to look up to you," a former TV co-worker once asked me. "Because I don't have to be on TV, or be anything in particular to feel special," I replied. "I am just as special running the sweeper as I am doing a TV segment in front of thousands of viewers," I told her.

I say all of this in humility, because to me, it is scary when someone places their entire identity on something as fleeting and superficial as being a celebrity. The truth is, I have tasted much glory in my life, but I have also lost just as much. I have won in karate tournaments, and I have lost in karate tournaments. I have gotten jobs of a lifetime, and I have lost jobs of a lifetime.

Through it all, I have realized that I am neither greater nor lesser of a person. I am still just who I am. I have learned to maintain my sense of self-worth, whether I am on the podium holding flowers, or not. As Kathy put it, "if you don't know who you are, somebody will always be around to tell you."

I take pride in knowing that, as a martial arts instructor, I am helping others complete their discovery of who they really are, especially when I hand them the sweeper. I agree with Kathy, who stood 6'7" tall in her high-heeled shoes. I will keep intact my sense of self-esteem always, regardless of what other people may think. I will be true to myself. If they have a problem with that, it is their problem, not mine.

Life Defined
Alexandra Allred

I was a very active kid growing up. My father was a U.S. Diplomat, so we lived all over the world. It was up to me to find my own entertainment. When you live in communist Russia as a kid, each time you go outside, a KGB agent follows you. There is no such thing as video games, or TV, and there are no shopping malls at which to hang out. You learn to play, "How to lose the KGB guy," and it is quite entertaining.

Because my father was a Diplomat, I lived in remote places such as Baghdad, Iraq, Tunis, Tunisia and Moscow, and I experienced firsthand the effects of discrimination and abuse against women and children. I eventually worked with U.N. officials to incorporate "Games for Girls" as part of their educational program to third world nations. Later, iParenting.com magazine nominated me for "Mom of the Year" for contributions to research in obstetrics and gynecology.

My dad liked to joke that each morning, somewhere in a dingy basement, the KGB agents were given their assignments for the day, and it was resolved with a game of "rock, paper, scissors" for who would get "the kid." I was a terror. I settled down a little when I was about 18. That is when I started taking martial art lessons, and I loved them.

Not much later, however, at the age of 19, I was the victim of a violent attack. Martial arts were my salvation. I never talk about this, but my assailant was a martial artist. Since then, I left martial arts, came back, left again, and then came back for good.

The martial arts empowered and excited me, and allowed me to reclaim "me" again. I was good, too. I only sparred with men for a long time, as I worked through some rage issues lingering from the attack. On a positive note, I began teaching, and loved it. At college, I taught and when the Kinesiology department heard about me, they asked me to student teach self-defense for a semester. I loved it. I began teaching self-defense to women on campus.

During this time, I realized the specific differences between men and women when it comes to self-defense. I said it before, and I will continue to say it. Men often do not understand how to teach self-defense to women. They do not understand that what works so simply for them does not, cannot, and will not work for a 5'2" petite woman who has never done a ki-hop in her life!

I could have let the wickedness I experienced with martial arts drive me away, but the essence of what martial arts were always drew me back. I believe that good will always prevail over bad. I continued and did very well. Harpers Bazaar magazine, Black Belt, and Redbook featured me in 1992 for teaching martial arts to U.S. State Department members. This occurred simultaneously at a time when I was committed and focused on another monumental task, training for the US women's bobsled team.

There is no doubt in my mind that my martial art background caught the attention of the U.S. Bobsled and Skeleton Federation (USBSF). I truly believe that my martial art training gave me the courage to try bobsled, even though I had never been in one in my life!

One day, I was watching ESPN and saw a bobsled. "Man, that's cool," I said. I waited and waited for the women bobsledders, until I realized there were none. I did some research and later found out that women were not allowed to bobsled because the sport was deemed "too powerful and too dangerous" for them.

I found this extremely interesting in relation to my martial art. When I was engaged in sparring, and excelling even against men, I could handle the danger and fast pace. I decided to protest for women bobsledders, even though I was not one. I wrote letter after letter, until I received a phone call essentially saying, "Hey, big mouth..." and that was how I was invited to the first ever women's try-outs.

I fought the long battle to have women's bobsledding included in the Olympic Games. Little by little, I made the cuts and reached the U.S. Nationals. The United States Olympic Committee named me athlete of the year for my sport. Even more than that, I was pregnant at the time. I know that my martial art background was the basis, not just for making the bobsled team, but also for everything that I did.

Later, while pregnant with my second child, I took part in a study with the renowned Dr. James Clapp III, on how extreme exercise affects the placenta. Dr. Clapp was particularly interested in me because there was very little data collected on sprint training, plyometrics, and heavy weight lifting for a pregnant woman. At five months pregnant, I was squatting 375 lbs. and clocked at 21 MPH on sprint drills. Both the United States and the International Olympic Committee for pregnant athletes still use my workout regimen.

In the late 90s, however, I left the martial arts world, discouraged and disappointed. At that time, I had seen too much. The "art" as I had known it inexplicably changed. Anyone could buy a belt.

I would watch as people passed belt exams, performing kicks that were almost unidentifiable. I watched people spar with very little control, with no method, and with very little skill. I was watching the art form that I loved so much, that saved my life, being bastardized into a joke. Therefore, I walked.

I later attended a kickboxing class in a very popular gym in Washington D.C. I was appalled and thought what are these people doing? I felt as if I was watching the Rockettes meet the Dallas Cowboy cheerleaders, with some spastic punching in between.

I went back home and approached my gym's manager, and I told him that I wanted to teach kickboxing that had real benefits beyond cardio. If you are going to dedicate yourself to something called kickboxing, should you not be able to kick your way out of paper bag? I have been doing it ever since.

I reached a point in my life and my career when I really wanted to give back, the way that martial artists should. I teach free self-defense classes twice a year, and everyone is welcome. I teach free kickboxing classes to special needs young adults. I want them to feel strong, empowered, and happy.

Many things in life come full circle, and it is no different for my life experiences. As for bobsledding, I eventually helped get women's bobsled in the Olympic Games. I was the first U.S. women's champion. I wrote the women's by-laws for the USBSF. I had some amazing experiences traveling on the World Cup.

While on assignment with *Sports Illustrated for Women*, I tried out for and earned a spot on a women's professional football team. Again, I found myself in a once male-only sport, and I wrote about the social ramifications of playing professional football as a woman.

Many of my life experiences have been interesting and different. I learned a lot from all of them, because I always pushed myself to follow my passions, and unearth opportunities for other women. Of all that I have been through, there is still only one experience that stands out as my very best learning experience, however, and that is my first black belt.

I was completely confident about earning my first black belt. I had it locked up! There was not one person in that dojo who could beat me in sparring. My forms were spot on. I was tight, strong, and fierce. I had my own small following, and I was already on schedule for taking over as instructor for some of the classes. I even had my black belt personalized and specially made for me. It was a done deal.

When I had to perform my forms, I felt good. It was easy. I could have performed the orange belt forms with my eyes closed! I have this, I was thinking in my mind. The next thought that went through my mind was not as reassuring, and was something like, "Oh, crap."

I went completely blank. The head instructor looked at me and told me to regroup, turn around, fix my uniform, and take a deep breath. I did that. I turned back. I was still blank. I failed in front of everyone.

Truly, walking into the exam, I thought I was ready to rock. Instead, I was blank in front of those who looked up to me. I could not remember my forms. It was awkward and embarrassing. No one knew what to say or do. I just sat back down and put on a brave face until I got home and cried. I was completely humiliated.

About 2:00 A.M., I woke up, got out of bed, and ran through all my katas in the dark. I still remember hearing my husband's voice in the dark when I was done ask, "Better?"

I had to wait two months to test again. Those months were the best and most horrible two months of my adult life. Through the disappointment and humiliation, I realized how much I really wanted and needed the black belt. I was humbled and eventually grateful. It turned out to be my best experience. I needed failure to succeed.

I went on to earn my second black belt while pregnant with my third child, and today I am a 4th degree black belt. I continue to teach martial arts, kickboxing, boxing, and Pilates at a community college and gym outside Dallas, Texas.

Incredible and varied experiences have filled my life. Along with the lifestyle I've described, I have also appeared in numerous publications, including, *Sports Illustrated, Muscle&Fitness, Hers, Self, Fit, Self Defense for Women, Shape, Good Housekeeping*, and *Redbook* magazines.

I appeared on USA Today, Dallas Morning News, and in the New York Times, and the Washington Post. I have appeared on NBC, have done blogging for NBC's coverage of the Olympic Games, and appeared on the *Ricky Lake Show*, CBS, NBC, ABC News affiliates, the Oxygen Channel, BBC and ABC Australia.

I have learned so many things since the days of my childhood, living in Russia. I have excelled in areas where women had no previous stake. I failed in front of others, but fought back hard enough to succeed. From here, I will continue moving forward to accept new challenges and pave new paths. I will always strive to make a difference.

One in a Million
Mary Moonen

Due to a knee and shoulder problem, my doctors told me a few years ago, that I should not continue practicing martial arts. I became discouraged and depressed and gave away my gear. I always believed that once a martial artist, always a martial artist. I so much wanted to continue, but I could not.

Teaching women's self-defense and martial arts to children were always my strong interests. I still wanted to participate in these activities so I decided to partner up with someone to continue. That is when I saw a van pass by with Master Kevin Bergquist's name on it.

I called him, and we met to discuss co-teaching. He asked why I was no longer practicing since I was already a brown belt. I explained why my injuries prevented me from continuing to study American Kempo.

He told me to come to his school, put on a gi, and do what I could do. He suggested that I modify, do fewer pushups, and keep kicks low. He gently guided me back. If not for him, I may have never returned.

Once I joined this dojo, I felt immediately like I was home. The only issue was that I was a brown belt, but looked a lot more like a lower rank because it had been so long since I trained. As mentioned, I already had some physical issues and limitations. I had a knee replacement and had to fix three tears in my rotator cuff and my bicep muscle. I also winded easily. He accepted that and helped me train.

Just after finishing sparring at the dojo in December 2013, I was excited to have superseded a personal goal of sparring longer than two minutes, by more than twenty seconds. I felt so damn good and happy. Unexpectedly, though, after going to sleep that night, I woke up with a crushing chest pain. I went to the hospital, but they sent me home with ice and pain medication, thinking it was a sparring injury to my sternum.

Still, I could not get comfortable. I was nauseous and by the next morning, I knew that something was wrong. ER tests immediately showed that I was having a medical cardiac event, and I had two stents put in. They sent me home, but while resting I felt something weird in my chest again. I returned to the hospital, and they put in another stent. I should have had it the first time, but discovered that the insurance would not cover three stents in that first visit.

My martial art training and mindset kicked in during these medical issues. I had to fight to get my message across that something was wrong. Doctors wanted to dismiss it as relating to martial art injuries, but I had to be clear and convince them otherwise. I had to use a quick reaction time and believe in myself to get the treatment that I needed, just as I had learned in martial arts.

The experience was very like a real defense situation. I had to assess, be situationally aware, and break through denial. Women often do not listen and follow their instinct, which is a part of awareness. Instinct told me that morning that I was having a heart attack. Instinct told me again to go back the second time. If not for my martial art training and mindset, things may have turned out differently.

While women learn to be nice, respectful, courteous, and to smile, boys duke out their differences on the playground. Martial arts taught me the other side of who I am. I spoke out and ask questions about my medical situation. I realized that if you are wrong, feel embarrassed, or hurt someone's feelings, you must still go with your gut reactions. Listen to your intuition. It worked for me.

After my heart attack, I started to listen to my body more than ever. I noticed some pain in my right lower quadrant in front. I thought maybe it was a kidney stone issue. There was no severe pain, yet I was trained to think proactively. If it was a stone, I needed a CT scan. To stay ahead of the pain, the same way I learned in martial arts to assess and be aware, I went for the scan.

Two years earlier, I was not as proactive a patient. I had gone to the ER for a very similar pain, and medical professionals told me that my appendix was enlarged. They chose not to remove it. They said that some people have "larger body organs" than others, and I believed them. I would later learn that you shouldn't believe everything the doctors say.

I should have advocated more. Who has an enlarged appendix? I had never heard of this. I went to a surgeon, but since it was not life threatening, insurance considered the surgery elective and would not pay for it.

This time around, though, when I went to the ER, the surgeon decided to take the appendix out. He removed it immediately. I did not like the doctor's bedside manner; he seemed very cold and abrupt. I had a bad vibe about him, but the surgery was an emergency.

While in the hospital, I had an allergic reaction to some medication. Again, I had to advocate for myself and prove through a photo I had taken earlier, that the reaction (hives) was there.

This was not the worst of my news, however. The diagnosis was not good. I had a rare cancer of the appendix. One in a million people have it. I had to use humor to cope. I always knew I was special, but one in a million?

I learned that a doctor who did not specialize in oncology would perform the surgery. When cancer is growing inside of you, it is scary, and you do not know what it means, but you know that you want it out of your body as soon as possible.

Because I am a proactive, high energy, "let's get this done" kind of person, I almost went along with the quickly scheduled surgery. Then, someone at a resource center reminded me of something very important. She said, "You have a rare cancer, and you haven't gotten a second opinion?" I left immediately, called the cancer center, and canceled the surgery.

They did a colonoscopy to see if the cancer spread to the colon, then a laparoscopy to look around. They originally thought they would take out pieces of the colon and intestine then put it back together. When they went in, they learned it had metastasized. They called it Stage 4. It sounded to me like end of life, but that was not really the case.

Nothing was easy after that. There was some confusion at first about chemotherapy schedules, but it finally worked out. I had to rely on more than just treatments, though, so I turned to my spirituality. I have always drawn my spirituality from different sources.

In karate, we sometimes start with meditation, or a quieting of the mind. In most martial arts seminars that I have taken, there is also a moment of silence and reflection. It is the chance to let go of your difficulties and and become grounded. I also listen to many meditational reflections. I know the importance of grounding the brain and clearing your mind. Like at the dojo, you must leave it all behind and stay in the present.

It is so important to be mindful in your practice, and not get ahead of yourself. When I find myself in negative self-talk, I think of drills and discipline from my martial art. I remember that I did ten pushups, which eventually led to a hundred before I realized it, and I met a goal that I did not think I could.

I also had to apply martial art mindset during these initial days of my diagnosis. You hear horrible stories about chemotherapy like hair loss and nausea. I wondered how I would get through it. I knew I had to remain grounded and leave negativity behind, so I recounted how I had finally achieved my black belt. This helps me get through anything.

My dojo is like a family, which is another way my martial art practice helped me. It is not an isolated school, but rather a place where we help each other. In a healthy dojo like this, there is no ego. There is collaboration, sharing, and teamwork. You need to be patient and gracious to teach and apply that kind of humility.

I had to face that this cancer was a lot bigger than I was. There was no way I could handle it alone. I knew I would need a boatload of help, but I did not want people to be overly dramatic either. I wanted to carry myself as a fighter, not a victim.

I set clear boundaries and asked others not to cross them. I asked visitors to text in advance before visiting me in the hospital. If they wanted to bring something, I told them I would rather receive a clipping from a garden or a plant, rather than balloons or flowers.

I forbid anyone to give me medical advice. Some still tried to impart their advice, against my wishes. One of them told me to "not poison" myself with chemo." This did not help me. I told them I was going to do exactly what the doctor said to do, and that I never wanted to hear the word "poison" again. Chemo, to me, is my "life saving" medication. Everyone must decide for himself what is best.

The biggest thing martial arts gave me is my voice for my choice. Part of turning 50 and having this cancer helped me understand I only have one life to live, and no one will dictate my life. The principles and codes of honesty and integrity that I learned in martial arts, apply.

As I go through treatments, it has gotten more difficult. After the initial chemotherapy effects, I bounced back. As treatments went on, however, my body took a toll, including horrible stomachaches, neuropathy in hands and feet (pain of walking on sharp rocks or shells), and cramping in my hands.

The surgery that I need to have is known as MOAS or "mother of all surgeries." It is a complicated and long surgery. During my recovery, I plan to stay in touch with my martial art friends.

The martial art community has lifted me up more than any other has. I am friends with many good people on social media who inspire me daily. All of them are brothers and sisters to me. These are the people I respect the most because we are all following the same traditions and expectations. They are a whole community of people who support and motivate me.

My martial art practice and my cancer are both journeys that have taught me how to overcome. I could have never fought this one-in-a-million cancer without being a one-in-a-million kind of martial arts woman.

Escape to America
Ccuong Tran "Kim" Weaver

Martial Arts have given me the mental, emotional, and physical strength, to survive and prosper through life's challenges. Through martial arts, I have come to know my inner self – the good parts and the not so good parts. They have made me a better person and someone with depth of character.

I take pride in encouraging women and children to speak their opinions and handle bullies in their lives. As I look to the future, I do so with the confidence that I can handle whatever life sends my way.

I am Kim Tran Weaver, designated Master, 5th Degree Black Belt in Korean Taekwon-Do and a certified Baptiste teacher of Power Vinyasa Yoga. I have been committed to physical fitness and martial arts for more than twenty years, and for the past two years in the Baptiste School of yoga. My life is empowered through these practices of mind, body, and spirit, as I continue my journey of physicality, personal development, and life transformation.

My physicality helped me put into perspective an early life in Vietnam, where panic, pain, and terror reined. After escaping on the last ship off the beach on April 30, 1975, I arrived in Atlanta, Georgia. There, I built my life of local and world community service, and my 30-year career in clothing design, and later, real estate. During that time, I studied Martial Arts, self-defense, several styles of tai chi, hapkihae myong mu kwan, and yoga.

My journey from Vietnam was very difficult, but molded me into who I am today. When living in the refugee camp at Phu Quoc Island on April 30, 1975, I heard the radio announcement that the North Vietnamese were victorious, and had won the war.

After the news, everyone began to panic. I came out of my shelter, and people were running everywhere. They were frightened and confused. It seemed as if they did not know what to do. In that moment, I began to understand that my life was changing forever.

I left our life in Vietnam by escaping with most of my family. We started on a long journey that ended in America. The experience was at times terrifying. I did not know where we would end up or what our life would be in the future.

Today, I think back to my memories of the war. Some have faded, but I always remember the date, and the few months it took for our escape to America. During this escape, there were a few hours when I thought everyone in my family would be killed. We stopped in the Philippines Islands, Guam and Wake Islands, Fort Chaffee Arkansas, and finally Atlanta, Georgia.

As a child of five or six years old in Vietnam, my life was not always filled with panic, pain, and terror, but the war was always all around us and never went away. My father worked for the government, so I had a better childhood than most. To avoid the communists, we moved many times. I always thought of Dieu Tri Quy Nhon, located near the ocean between North and South Vietnam, as my hometown.

I was the third oldest of nine children, and I had a lot of responsibility. As I got older, I became more aware of the war. One night our village was attacked. This is one of my first memories. We heard a loud boom that knocked our front door open.

My mother screamed at us to follow her and ordered us to get down on our hands and knees. We had to crawl through a hole to the back of the house, previously dug to protect the family from the big guns. That night it was filled with rainwater up to my neck.

My father was not at home, because almost every night he had to sleep in a different house. At daylight, I realized that the next-door neighbor's house had burned down. Many times, because of my father's job, we had to move to different towns that had more protection. There were constant curfews.

On March 2, 1975, we were at Cam Rahn Bay. I went outside to mail a letter to a friend and saw no one else around. That meant we had to leave again. We were unable to find my father, but someone said he was at Cam Rahn Bay beach. We gathered our belongings and went to the beach, but could not find him.

My mother cried, and we did not know what to do. Suddenly, we saw a large raft coming towards the beach. My mother begged the raft's owner to take us to the big American ship offshore. He said no because the raft had no engine and was not big enough, but he eventually allowed us to get in. He took us further from the beach to find a bigger boat.

We had to leave everything at the beach that we had brought with us, except a few family mementos and the clothes we were wearing. As we paddled away from the beach, the waves got bigger and bigger, and the boat almost turned upside down. We thought we would all die any minute.

Then we saw a bigger boat come closer to us. This one was a fishing boat with an engine. Mom begged him to take the family to the ship and said she would pay all the money he needed. He said he would, but warned that it would be very dangerous.

The waves got bigger as we got closer to the ship. Finally, we made it. When we looked up, we were shocked and happy to see father at the railing of the ship. He called people to pull us up. The ship was crowded, and there were people everywhere. There was no food, and we had to sleep in an exposed place on the deck where we got wet when it rained. It was miserable, but better than the alternative.

We were there for several weeks. The Red Cross brought some food, but gang members stole most of it. We received some potatoes to eat that were rotten and full of salt from the water. One time I had to wait in line for hours, but there was nothing to buy even though I had money.

In the end, my family was scattered. My oldest sister had the chance to go with us but chose to stay in Vietnam to take care of grandfather and big brother. The rest of us ended up at the refugee camp at Phú Quốc Island for several weeks.

When we heard the announcement of the North Vietnamese victory announced April 30, I was shocked to see guns, uniforms, and military equipment of all types everywhere. The soldiers had stripped to help them avoid capture. Everyone there fled to a beach where several small boats were taking the people to Vietnamese and American ships anchored offshore. It was a time of sheer chaos.

Once again, we could not find my father and my mother panicked. She decided to be the family leader, gathered my siblings and me together, and followed the crowd towards the beach. Several thousands of us walked two hours then saw the beach filled with many more people, small fishing boats, rowboats, and canoes.

Among the crowd, we found my father wandering around. He was happy to see all of us at the beach because he was as worried about us, as we were about him.

At that time, no one took the currency. My mother had sewn gold jewelry into her clothing. She used a lot of the gold to buy room on the last small boat to take us to the big Vietnamese navy ship offshore. By this time, it was midnight. The people without money were left on the beach to face the communist terror.

Once the boat was a few miles from the beach, the engine stopped. We knew we would die if we returned to the beach because the communists were in control and wanted my father. My father found a friend on another small boat. Then, we found a big ship ten to fifteen miles offshore. When we made it to the ship, the sailors pulled us on board by ropes. They pulled some of my younger siblings up in baskets. It was difficult to hold onto the ropes.

My family all made it to the top of the ship. Sadly, many other people in boats that night could not hold onto the ropes and fell into the water and drowned. Long after midnight, I lay on the deck looking at the stars. I realized that I would never be going back home. I would never see my friends, grandfather, older sister, or big brother again.

The navy ship took us to the Philippine Islands, where we switched to an American commercial ship that took us to Guam. At Guam, we lived in tents, had medical exams, took English lessons, and even learned about credit cards. After staying about two months in Guam, we were taken to Wake Island for five days and then to Fort Chaffee, Arkansas.

Fort Chaffee was a military base and refugee camp. For three months, I attended classes to learn English taught by the University of Arkansas. The whole time in Arkansas, a refugee organization searched for someone to sponsor us. Finally, a Presbyterian church in Atlanta, Georgia sponsored us. The church helped us rent a house and helped my father and I find jobs.

By the time I was seventeen years old, and the oldest sibling, I worked five days a week in a factory, and Saturdays at a wedding dress shop to help support the family. My siblings continued their education although I was unable to continue mine.

Although life was not easy for me in America, words could not describe how I felt about my freedom. It was wonderful. My older sister survived with her family. She found our big brother who survived years of communist indoctrination, and now lives in a suburb of Atlanta. I have wonderful children and see most of my siblings. Each person in my family has different story about April 30, 1975, and about what has happened in their lives since. However, these words are mine, and this is my story on how I escaped to America.

POSITIVE & SPIRITUAL WARRIORSHIP

When obstacles arise, you change your direction to reach your goal; you do not change your decision to get there.
Zig Ziglar

Ho'oponopono
Michelle Manu

Today in the Hawaiian culture, the Kahunas (priests and wise men/women) still use a spiritual practice called Ho'oponopono. Ho'oponopono means to correct or set the spirit right. The Hawaiian warriors practiced this daily along with Lua, Hula, making weaponry, chiropractic medicine, and massage.

Ho'oponopono involves taking continual inventory of one's spiritual life in its entirety. The process involves identifying people, places, and events that connect you through the emotions of regret, grief, shame, anger, fear, pride, chronic or reoccurring illness, and depression.

They believe that everything is energy and that all of life (everything!) is connected. This includes our individual consciousness connected to the collective consciousness at the energetic level. Personal healing emerges as collective healing for all (wo)mankind. Our basic emotional states transmit themselves to the universe, which affects acts of God.

It is my belief that spirit is first, mind is second, and physical is last. A thought is energy, energy becomes a thing, and that thing is either life giving, or life depleting. Ho'oponopono is the letting go process to be free to live in peace and self-evolve.

From an early age, everyone learns what is good and what is bad. Crossing the street without looking is bad. Finishing all your food is good. As a young woman, it is most likely wise for your safety and survival to follow general guidelines of what is good and bad. As adults, we apply them subjectively based upon our unconscious and reinforced mental programming, through previous experiences.

We must consider at what point these good and bad classifications hinder our ability to take wise and brave chances. How can we step forward and creatively choose what we wish to experience?

This is where the internal predator resides, and frequently tortures the psyche. She controls our endless thoughts, paralyzes us, and robs us of the place, space, territory, and time to create forward movement, and/or get unstuck. This is the fear-based condemning voice and negative self-talk that everyone hears in his or her mind.

In this negative state, a woman loses her energy to create, whether it be solutions to mundane matters in her life, such as school, family, friendships, or her concerns with compelling issues in the larger world. It affects her issues of spirit, such as her personal development or her martial art.

This is not a mere procrastination, for it continues over weeks and months of time. She seems "flattened out, filled with ideas perhaps, but deeply anemic and more and more unable to act upon them." Clarissa Pinkola Estes, Ph.D., *Women Who Run with the Wolves*

How do we get to this point of taking our existence and ourselves more seriously each day? It is through what we have been holding on to, not necessarily by acquiring new information. Rather, it is the letting go of the unnecessary and non-useful on to which we have been holding.

It is no longer useful, although it did once serve a purpose. It is like the sun shining. The sun is always shining and does not discriminate about upon whom it shines. It is our duty to remove the clouds, or obstacles, that remain in our way.

If obstacles are deemed as opportunities, then they become a maximum opportunity for growth at the perfect time. We have all had moments of "Why didn't I do this sooner?" or, "I should have known this already." This is nonsense! Everything awaits the time for when we can recognize it, and become aware of what has always been.

For some reason, we are now in the process of understanding this. It is the time to receive this revelation, so do not allow the predator to tell you that you have done anything wrong.

Sigmund Freud said in classical psychoanalysis, that the repressed impulse or feeling was to be neutralized, sublimated, socialized, and channeled into constructive drives of love, work and creativity. Martial arts are an act of love, courageous work on internal and external Self, and creativity in form and non-form, in preparation to defend Self and others. All forms of martial arts help with stress identification, management, and self-confidence. The real source of "stress" is internal.

David R. Hawkins, MD, Ph.D. says that there is no such thing as stress, that there is only stressful thinking in the mind of the thinker. We cannot bottle stress and examine it. It is unseen. To identify and manage, the thinker must look at what the thinker believes is stressful. How do we identify, let go, and remove the clouds? He says, "Letting go involves being aware of a feeling, letting it come up, staying with it, and letting it run its course without wanting to make it different or do anything about it."

It means simply to let the feeling be there, and to focus on letting out the energy behind it. The first step is to allow yourself to have the feeling without resisting it, venting it, fearing it, condemning it, or moralizing about it. It means to drop judgment, and to see that it is just a feeling. This technique is to go with the feeling and surrender all efforts to modify it in any way.

Let go of wanting to resist the feeling, resistance that keeps the feeling going. When you cease resisting, or trying to modify the feeling, it will shift to the next feeling accompanied by a lighter sensation. If you do not resist the feeling, it will disappear as the energy behind it dissipates.

To surrender means to have no strong emotion about a thing. It is okay if it happens, and it is okay if it does not. When we are free, there is a letting go of attachments. We can enjoy a thing, but we do not need it for our happiness. There is a progressive diminishing of dependence on anything or anyone outside of ourselves. These principles are in accord with the basic teachings of Buddha to avoid attachments to worldly phenomena, as well as basic teaching of Jesus Christ to "be in the world but not of it." David R. Hawkins, MD, Ph.D., *Letting Go: The Pathway of Surrender*

Sometimes we surrender and let go of a feeling and it reappears and persists. It just keeps coming up! You have not done the process wrong nor have you failed, but there is more of it you must surrender.

"Another block that may occur is the fear that if we let go of a desire for something, we won't get it. It is often beneficial to look at some commonly held beliefs and let go of them right in the beginning, such as: (1) We only deserve things through hard work, struggle, sacrifice, and effort; (2) Suffering is beneficial and good for us; (3) We don't get anything for nothing; and (4) Things that are very simple aren't worth much." David R. Hawkins, MD, Ph.D., *Letting Go: The Pathway of Surrender*

Not all lessons or revelations need to be core shaking or painful, or make us aware of our fears, pain, disappointments, or a new fork in the path. Letting go is a much more peaceful way to exist. It allows you to let yourself and others off the hook, by silencing the internal predator, and graduating from "knowing about" to undisputable "knowingness" at your core.

This is where we thrive and empower womankind. A good analogy would be teaching martial arts and women's self-defense. The student has incorrect, therefore, ineffective technique. She can see and feel the non-verbal discontent with herself. You instruct and encourage her to believe in herself, focus, and try again.

In her work, she gains real-life experience in graduating from knowing about, to knowingness, as she perfects her movements. She leaves training with a taller stance, immovable confidence, and has a new cannot-be-dimmed twinkle in her eye. No one can take this from her. Only she can rob herself. This newfound strength will bleed into every area of her life and with those with whom she crosses paths. The ripple begins, and she influences other women.

All the Great Masters point us within. This is the core of martial arts. "Be like water," "Be of no mind," "Be prepared for all things," "Be of good intent." Become the virtues you seek, to attract and develop in other spirits.

Who is the woman in the mirror? Who would you like the woman in the mirror to be? Everything can change in a snap second; you just need to decide on it. Straight and narrow is the path. Waste no time. Hold back nothing.

This is a helpful grounding prayer and meditation by healer Kim Pentecost. I do this daily at bedtime: "I acknowledge, bless, release, and transmute all that I have taken in that does not match the truth of my heart in love and only love, through all time, space, dimension and reality. In addition, I receive pure love through and through all that I am, from all that is love and only love. A Ho (So Be It or Amen)"

I Want to Be a Warrior
Andrea Harkins

I do not know exactly what it means to be a warrior. I have an expectation that it would include traditions, honor, respect, and discipline. You probably have your own vision of a warrior, depending on your upbringing, the movies you have seen, your training, or your literacy in the martial arts.

The important thing about the warrior is not so much how he looked, or what he did. It is more about his attributes and values. We view him with awe because these traits are not easy to attain. When I equate martial arts with warrior concepts, they remind me how far off the mark I am in my daily trek, yet, I continually seek to find my way.

You make decisions every single day. They include what to wear, what to say, when to smile, who to like, where to go, and how to feel. It is almost mundane to make these decisions every day. Why, then, can we not make other small but important decisions about being more warrior-like in our lives, treat each other well, or behave properly?

Do you wonder if you could ever be a modern-day warrior? Could you be brave, courageous, and willful? When I asked myself this warrior question, what I am really asking is if I would do anything to save myself, my children, or those I love.

The quickness and clarity of my answer surprised me. I would do anything to save those I love. This unrecognized warrior's spirit sits deeply within me. I am ready and willing to defend that which I love, and nothing will ever change that. It is not a choice or a decision, it just is.

Still, there is more to being a warrior than seeking super-strong positive attributes. The warrior spirit breaks down in society because not everyone strives for personal excellence.

Many are happy with complacency. I warn against complacency because it compromises every inch of warrior spirit that you have. Each person must strive for excellence, and seek his potential. Anything less is a personal disservice, and a stifling of the intricate martial art spirit that should flourish.

I am not exempt from lack of motivation and direction. I waited a very long time in my life before I decided to apply myself, or to pursue a strong and passionate personal mission. Now, I realize now that I was meant to inspire others through my martial art mindset and writing.

Now, I strive to be productive and successful, while at the same time support the endeavors of others. I over-commit at times, yet, I find the results to be worthwhile. I am fighting to cultivate a warrior environment for us all because I know that you and I can rise above the ordinary. We will stand out as dedicated and committed individuals who create positive energy.

You have a great opportunity to create your own traditions and heritage using a warrior spirit as a guide. Right now is a good time to indulge in a positive and rewarding renewal of self. When your desire to make some positive change in your life has been lingering in the back of your mind, that is the time for you to take the steps to rise above.

A martial artist is a role model and warrior. Children look at my black belt and ask if I am a master. Women my age assume that I am wise. Men find the juxtaposition of femininity and power intriguing. Everyone has an expectation that there is something very special about me, and that is my call to warriorship.

There was a time when I wondered if I could live up to this expectation of warriorship, or if the responsibility was too big to carry. The answer is, I can and I will. I am ready to apply the warrior attributes of tradition, honor, respect, and discipline, to my life. I need to practice what I preach, and I still have a long, long way to go. The journey is just beginning. There is no doubt, though. I want to be a warrior.

The Power of Positivity
Dana Hee

In the realm of Hollywood, there are two definites. If you focus on the positive, your chances for success will multiply. If you focus on the negative, or your fears, you will fail. Failure takes on a completely new meaning when you are performing a death-defying stunt!

"Today, I need you to stunt double this entryway guard to Paramount Studios," my boss told me on the set of the 'Martin Short' TV show. "Mike here will crash his car through the guard barrier rail into the parking lot. You will then rush after him along the sidewalk here. As you catch up to the car, you will pop up onto this fire hydrant, and then throw yourself onto the roof of his car. There you will hang on, pounding on the roof for him to stop."

"Sure, no problem," I responded. I thought to myself how fascinating it was that he did not tell me of this very dangerous gag when he first hired me! Then I reminded myself, Ahhh well. Welcome to my life. You chose this career. Time to 'man-up,' Dana!

We rehearsed the timing, and we "dialed in" the speed so that the car was in place beside me as I jumped onto the fire hydrant. We both knew the timing was critical. If I jumped too soon, I could end up in front of the car and under the wheels. If I jumped too late, I would miss the only opportunity to grasp the open windowsills for leverage, and avoid ending up on the ground. They were two undesirable choices.

The first time we filmed, there was an element of doubt in my mind. Yet on hearing "Action!" I raced to the fire hydrant as Mike drove the car along. The timing was exactly as planned, but as I popped up onto the hydrant, I allowed my doubt to interfere. Maybe I am too early! I thought to myself.

I hesitated just a beat, and then threw myself onto the car. Only now, my momentum had stalled out, and I landed too late. I grabbed wildly for the roof before bouncing down onto the trunk, the bumper, and then to the pavement.

You can bet the next time the camera rolled, I kept my focus completely on nailing this stunt by committing my mind 110% to its success. Success is much more fun than failing! In fact, success can appear to be much easier than the underlying difficulty in achieving it.

I love the power of positivity. It helps me overcome fear. It keeps me on track. It helps to eliminate some of the potential disasters on the road to success!

You must expect great things of yourself before you can do them.
Michael Jordan

The Martial Art Dream
Andrea Harkins

From the late 1980's through the late 1990's, I studied martial arts at a local community center. It was a great time of learning. Back then, there was no Internet from which to learn. You went to class and tried to keep up with the skills and techniques that you learned so you could excel.

The aim for me was not just belt progression. Camaraderie and cultivation of friendships were important. The women supported each other. They bonded because they had the patience to rehearse thoroughly, which contrasted with some of the men. Most of the instructors were men, simply because there were not as many women practicing.

The energy thrived when everyone warmed up and practiced together. The coordinated swish of uniforms during practice was like a single, timed breath that drew everyone together in a tightly woven community. I learned not just from one instructor, but also from many. They were all helpful, encouraging, and supportive.

During my first pregnancy, I continued attending classes the entire time, and had a lot of encouragement. I was surprised at how little my growing belly affected me. I did not do any falling, but my desire to continue and my momentum only slowed slightly. I recall sitting on the floor and trying to touch my toes, which got progressively more difficult during the months that passed, yet, I did not stop trying. That kind of determination stuck with me my entire life.

The area in which we practiced was a big open floor, not a fancy dojo. There were so many different people in attendance that you could literally work with different partners in stretching, drills, and one-step techniques and escapes. Without the internet, the student had the burden of learning. You had to pay attention, take notes, and practice, to progress. Nothing came easy or for free.

I grew into myself as a puppy grows into its paws, and I felt like I was a part of something special. My attendance at these classes turned me from a woman into a martial artist. I never let go of the martial art dream, of being a martial artist for life, and it never let go of me.

Dreams are not easy to follow. There is usually resistance from within, or from others. You must believe in yourself, and you have to pursue your dreams, no matter how difficult it may feel. When you stop asking yourself in what direction you want to go, then you remain the same or fall behind. You will wake up one day and realize that you denied yourself the chance to experience your personal truth.

Walking through the door to the martial art school on the very first day, you recognize some of your goals. You want to learn self-defense, or earn a black belt, or learn to fight.

You should address the options in your life. Open the door to life. Step through the threshold. Do not wander aimlessly. Some dreams open when you take the first step. Taking the first step into the dojo helped me turn my training into a personal mission of truth and dedication. A dream can start from a seed, and grow into an amazing accomplishment.

Today, my martial art dream sustains me and helps me break through personal barriers of all types. It carries me when I am weak and uncertain and allows me to grow in athleticism and opportunity. This prominently defines who I am today. I have learned to combine my martial art with my spirituality in a way that strengthens me two-fold. At any given time, I have one of these on my side, usually both.

You must always be aware of who you are. You may be busy with a family, or you may be tired or ill. None of that is a reason to give up the spirit that lives within you and guides you. Keep your dreams alive in your heart and mind until you have a chance to begin, or to accomplish them.

A long time ago, in a great big room at a community center surrounded by martial artists, I began a journey and a vision. That first day I had no thoughts of becoming a black belt. Yet, I knew I was in the right place. Because of my martial art beliefs, I will continually seek ways to improve using whatever time and resources I have.

Dreams are not always what you expect, or what you think you want, initially. They evolve and before you know it, you must decide to pause or pursue. If you choose to pause, you may never return. You take the risk when you push a dream aside.

If you pursue, even by just keeping your dream alive in your heart and mind, then one day you will see it come to fruition. You will always be thankful you made the right choice. To excel, achieve, and become the person you want to be, always believe in your martial art dream.

Something More about Colleen Davis
Andrea Harkins

A karateka who lives in South Africa, Colleen Davis, contacted me after reading my blog. She is a martial artist who had breast cancer at the time she wrote to me. She explained in her initial e-mail how she loved martial arts and wanted to continue her life as normally as possible during her cancer battle.

What is most intriguing about Colleen is not her cancer journey, but how she combines her spirituality and her martial art together, to become the strongest woman that she can. In her initial correspondence, she explained how her martial art mindset and her spirituality was in full swing, and how it carried her through her most desperate times. When she could not physically practice, she desperately missed it.

After her treatments, she slowly returned to her art. She participated in a martial art competition when she was still in recovery and physically too weak. She did not care about winning as much as she cared about having a goal, and something to which to look forward. In between when she sent her e-mail, and her return to her practice, Colleen had a lot to overcome.

Over the course of time, Colleen wrote me several very beautiful and expressive e-mails about her journey. It was in December 2014, when she introduced herself as a karate practitioner from South Africa. Here is the initial e-mail I received from her:

"Hi there. I just wanted to thank you for blogging. I remember when I first started karate. I was very thirsty for information and wanted to test myself about what I was learning and wanted more and more. My poor sensei had about two questions a day from me, which he wisely answered through teaching and never directly answering. Those were frustrating years. I have grown more silent and inward looking now that I have gained shodan, but as an adult learner, I still go on my own quests for knowledge.

I think as women, we are better at martial arts than when we are older because we no longer care what others think. I was interested in your article "karate-ka on the side" where you mentioned cancer. Was this a personal journey or just an example?

The reason I am asking is that I have to take a break from karate for a short while to fight my own battle. What I find interesting is that I am going deeper in my karate journey, using a lot more self-reflection, and doing more of kata and kihon in my head. I might have to forgo competition kumite due to reconstruction, but will cross that path when I get to it."

Since then, Colleen and I have corresponded back and forth during her cancer treatments. To say that she is an ordinary woman is an understatement. Dealing with cancer is devastating, but for karateka Colleen, it is just another necessary journey to discover who she really is. She is a practitioner and a competitor. She uses martial arts and faith as the basis of her experiences, and builds off both.

What is so touching about Colleen is her sturdy belief system. She readily applies martial arts concepts to her cancer fight. She shared some of her intimate insights from her martial art/cancer story.

In September 2014, she graded to Shodan in a National grading in South Africa JKA. At the age of 40, she was training four times a week for the South Africa JKA Championship. She mentally practiced karate throughout the day.

It was difficult sacrificing her roles as mother and wife, but her practice was a time in which she could be herself. It made her a better, happier person. She was challenged, fit, and healthy.

In early 2014, Colleen's life changed drastically, when she discovered a lump in her breast. Her mother was diagnosed with breast cancer two years earlier, and there was a family history of it on all sides. She knew on a subconscious level that this was not just a cyst, but convinced herself that it was nothing.

In November 2014, Colleen's diagnosis was Invasive Ducta Carcinoma Stage 1, Grade 3. It was an emotional time, as she had to turn her attention away from her martial art practice toward herself. Training for the last time in the dojo in 2014, she was strong and fully committed. With bittersweet intent, she said goodbye to the dojo, in preparation for her cancer treatments. She was encouraged by other cancer survivors who practiced martial arts, who could return to their practice. This gave her hope and strength for her challenge.

Colleen's descriptions of her journey are riveting. She says that a diagnosis of cancer "plucks you from wherever you are in your life, and places you in a fast-flowing river, in which the only control you have is how you mentally deal with the journey."

She had two operations, one to remove sentinel nodes out of her armpit, and a week later, a single mastectomy with an expander inserted. When she went into surgery, she was remarkably relaxed. "I had a wall of prayer and had a heavenly calmness around me," she shares.

In January, she started chemotherapy because her test results showed an aggressive cancer with an intermediate chance of returning within a few years. She decided that she would not think of herself as sick. She considered herself a woman with cells that had "rebelled, and she had to kill them before they killed her." She viewed chemotherapy as poison she had to take to kill the cells.

The chemotherapy treatments left her feeling tired, sick, and with weak joints. Her brain was in a fog and her mouth got sores. She also used kata as a gentle way of keeping her body and brain in a healthy space. Kata done in a slow gentle way was meditative and kept her feeling somewhat normal. She could not remember half of the katas she was supposed to know, even though she had done them for years, yet, her mindful practice gave her something to think about other than her treatment.

Chemotherapy was not just physically debilitating, it was also a mental drain. It took a lot of energy and self-actualization to get her body and mind ready for the side effects of the treatments. The night before beginning her second round of chemotherapy, she went to the dojo to make her mind strong. She was very weak and could not do much, but she found that she was still supple and could do mild kumite. She continually reminded herself that she was strong mentally, and told herself that she was not sick.

To carry on the self-image that she was not sick, she wore an ice cap for 3 hours while chemo treatments were in progress, to keep her hair. They were like having brain freezes.

She learned to relax when medical interventions were painful. She thought of difficult kata and practiced it in her head. Her body would relax, and only part of her brain was aware of the pain. Two weeks after her final chemotherapy session, she returned to the dojo.

She was weak and unfit, but it felt as if she had not been away. Her sensei was nice enough to tell her that it looked like she had not been away for four months, which gave her hope. She entered the championship competition as a personal challenge.

She had to relearn many of the upper belt kata, and had to choose a specific kata for the final. After discussion with her sensei, she decided on a powerful kata that contained only 24 moves, because she felt she could learn it in one month's time.

She was only training twice a week, and her strength seemed to be returning quickly. Twelve weeks to the day, after her last chemotherapy session, she competed in the elite veteran's division. She did not get a medal, but she did not embarrass herself either.

Unfortunately, she was aware that her passion for kumite was ending. She believed that reconstructive surgery was too expensive to mess with. The competition fulfilled her. She says, "This is what karate is, a personal journey of mental, physical and spiritual discovery. If you only compete for a competition, you will always be last year's champion. There is never an end to what you can learn about yourself or the art of karate."

Colleen Davis is a martial art woman who considers karate a lifeline. She used it when she experienced this difficult emotional and physical change in her life, and in her body. At age 40, she went straight into menopause. She was anxious about it at first because "We live in a world that is focused on youth and dismisses aging," she shares. "There is a lot of help for girls going through puberty and through the middle years, but menopause is not talked about." She takes an estrogen blocker that affects every system in her body, including her joints.

She realizes now that menopause is not as bad as she thought it would be. Because she practices an art that strengthens her mentally and physically, she is happy with who she is, and where she is. That is the key to life – being comfortable in your own skin.

She says, "I have a strong body and a strong mind as I travel through my life journey. I appreciate the benefits karate provides for me, to learn more about myself, to challenge myself, and to be centered. I am grateful for the journey and for the people who I have met. I am learning and enjoying every lesson life and karate is teaching me."

Colleen's love for her practice is evident in her demeanor, mindset, and actions. After returning to her practice, she sent me these words of wisdom. "I have just been at karate. Before, I felt flat, heavy and tired. Now I feel alive and sweaty, but happy. Actually, it has been a difficult road to get back, as I grapple with being unfit and having had a few months of comfort eating.

I think that women see karate as something more than most men. For us, it is a part of our battle with ourselves. All women battle with themselves, but in martial arts we get to really confront our personal thoughts and be free to be something more."

The Warrior Lifestyle
Jenny Sikora

The profound morality, integrity, and philosophy behind martial arts and the warrior lifestyle began to fascinate me when I was around 6 years old. I told both of my parents in 1986 that I wanted to apply the ethics and values of martial arts, and especially the warrior lifestyle, to my life.

I'm sure that both of my parents thought that my decision and fascination was just a phase. As I got older, they discovered that my decision was firm. My mother had a difficult time accepting my mindset. She was convinced that this lifestyle wasn't appropriate for girls or women. She tried to find me new hobbies that she felt were more suitable for a girl, per her own thinking, beliefs, and religion (Polish Catholic), but I had already made up my mind.

I knew one thing. I did not want to end up living the same kind of life as my mother, with restrictions and limited thinking. I wanted to show my mother, and the other women in my family, how much a woman could achieve, if her mind is not limited.

The first two women in my entire family who accepted my decision one-hundred percent, and encouraged my life philosophy, were my two grandmothers. They both found my beliefs and independence to be refreshing and rebellious, and a huge positive step in the right direction for the women in our family. Shortly afterwards, both of my grandmothers transitioned from being normal Polish, Catholic housewives, and stay home mothers, to finding jobs to make their own living and stand on their own two feet. My choices influenced my family.

In the beginning, it was not the martial arts training, the self-defense, or the ability to fight that caught my attention. It was the profound and essential wisdom, philosophy, values, morals, and principles of martial arts that influenced me. Loyalty, commitment, honor, honesty, courage, justice and integrity, were the very attributes I wanted for my life. These were the catalysts to aligning my actions and words with this life philosophy. What intrigued me the most was the fact that a true warrior always fights for what she believes.

As the years went by, the warrior vision and philosophy started to shape my beliefs, and they had a huge influence and impact on my opinions, views, priorities, behaviors, and actions. My fascination and interest in martial arts, and the warrior lifestyle, helped me grow from a child and teenager into an independent, confident, and mature adult.

Having an interest in this specific lifestyle and philosophy from such an early age, turned out to be a huge advantage through my school years. It kept me from making the same mistakes or poor decisions that many young people, especially girls, make. The martial art and warrior lifestyle prevented me from becoming a follower of classmates or friends, and instead, a leader of my own path and journey.

I remember how proud I was during my school years, because I was not afraid to stand out from the rest, speak my mind, or share my own ideas. I wanted to show my girlfriends that there was so much more to being a girl than just looking beautiful for the boys, or acting stupid and unintelligent to get attention.

Because of my philosophies and actions, I gained respect during those years from my teachers and classmates, especially the boys, and the other older students. Even then, my fascination for martial arts and the warrior lifestyle helped me avoid some of the normal teenage phases that many of the other girls faced.

Living the martial art and warrior lifestyle throughout these years really opened my eyes and prepared me for today's world. I couldn't understand why so many women in different communities around the world set such low expectations for themselves. I wondered why many blindly followed the rules of a system that lacked true principles, morally correct values, and decency.

In college, I began to study psychology, religion, history, and later the law, because I wanted to make a difference in people's lives. I felt the desire to teach important values by sharing the wisdom and philosophy of martial arts and the warrior lifestyle. I also wanted to help guide women, especially those with strict religious backgrounds, and make them aware of what it truly means to be a woman of vision and integrity.

I decided to combine these philosophies together, along with the basic practices of psychology, into coaching and mentoring. In the beginning, when I told my colleagues about combining these systems together, they thought that I was kidding, or that I had lost my mind. I didn't care. I had so much faith in the idea that I resigned from that position a few months later. I wasn't even allowed to practice my theoretical vision with the martial arts and the warrior lifestyle philosophy during my karate practice.

About two months after leaving my old job in 2011, I started my own small practice that offered people a new and different kind of lifestyle coaching and mentoring. In this same year, I came across a series of books on wisdom and warriorship for the very first time. After reading some of these books, I realized how awesome and inspiring they were. I liked the fact that the philosophies were refreshing, open, and honest.

I decided to include these books in some of my classes and lectures to see how my clients would react. The reaction was positive, just as I thought it would be. Both women and men could relate. They provide my clientele with great guidance, motivation, teaching, and reading material.

For many years now, my own childhood fascination and interest in martial arts and the warrior lifestyle philosophy have helped me grow and develop into being a person of whom I am truly proud. They have helped me overcome different obstacles and personal challenges in my life. The importance of the martial arts, the warrior lifestyle, and the whole warrior code of ethics, were exactly what I wanted to use in my life vision and philosophy.

My interest in martial arts began when I was in my late twenties after one of my girlfriends was beaten on the streets on her home from a party. After that, I convinced her that we needed to participate in self-defense class. That turned out to be a wise decision, because a few years later in 2011, a man tried to attack me during the evening, near my own apartment.

Because I had learned the basic moves and techniques in self-defense (street fight and kickboxing), my attacker was not able to hold me down, or drag me away. The martial art and warrior philosophy also helped me to remain focused and not panic in this situation.

In late 2012, I made the decision to try another martial art that had fascinated me for a couple of years, Capoeira. I always found this fusion of combat and dance fascinating. In this martial art, you use your body's agility and strength. An injury in my left wrist and hand a few months later forced me to take a break.

A year later, still dealing with some problems with my left wrist and hand, I had to consider other alternatives in martial arts. My interest in Shaolin Kung Fu developed more and more, so I decided to try it. As result, I earned a green belt. In the meanwhile, I still wanted to return to Capoeira training, even though almost three years had passed. I had to be mindful of my injury, but a true warrior never gives up. In October 2015, I returned to my Capoeira training.

My journey of martial arts and warriorship is never-ending. I continue to be alert to my desire to follow this path. From the beginning, I knew that I would use martial arts and warriorship for a greater purpose. Through my coaching, I can provide great examples of these valuable life lessons for others, as well.

I am happy that I had the opportunity to contribute and write a chapter for this book about martial arts and warriorship. I'm truly honored to share some of my own experiences and insights on martial arts and the warrior lifestyle philosophy.

The successful warrior
is the average person,
with lazer-like focus.
Bruce Lee

Don't Do Nothing
Pam Neil

My name is Pam Neil and I am 79 years old. I started martial arts (karate) at the age of 61, mostly because it was something I always wanted to do to get stronger and build self-confidence. Age has never been a factor, but rather a motivation. If anything, it gives me a competitive spirit.

When I started training in karate at the National Karate Schools of Chicago, I was smitten with the workout ethic. At first, it seemed quite daunting, even though I was fit, but soon I got into the rhythm of kicking, punching, blocking, and sparring. Sparring made me tougher, especially after receiving a kick to the head! After that, I learned to block. It all keeps you humble.

I have found, through the years, that learning karate and receiving a black belt is one of the most rewarding things that has ever happened to me. I have attained self-confidence, self-assurance, and abilities such as round, side, ax and jump kicks, which I never thought I could do, but I persevered.

Martial arts are not easy. You must keep going, even when you think you cannot any more, and then some. The rewards for your effort are that you become proud and happy at the same time.

The reason I still practice karate at my age is that I now have the ability and knowledge to keep going. One of my favorite things to do in karate is board breaks. I enter tournaments twice a year and usually get first or second place.

It is never too late to gain the benefits of exercise, whether you are looking for muscle tone, muscle building, or joint loosening. Emotional benefits of starting an active lifestyle at any age, include feeling better from the release of stress and tension, decrease depression and increase self-confidence. Osteoporosis and balance problems also decrease. Much of the aging I see is a decline due to prolonged inactivity.

I am also inspired by working side by side with my daughter Jacky, who is also a 4th degree black belt, as well as my granddaughter, Morgan, who is a 2nd degree black belt. It is a great opportunity for us to practice as female martial artists, together.

I also became a karate teacher. I have taught a senior women's self-defense course, and will be teaching more for the local Park Districts. I also help teach at the National Karate School and judge in the National Karate tournaments.

My journey into the black belt "sisterhood" has never completely defined me. However, it has enhanced me. I have not become aggressive, but more confident. I am prouder of myself now than before becoming a black belt. Now that I am a 4th degree I am not only proud, but I love to encourage women to take up a martial art. I want them to feel as confident as I do. I teach a self-defense course to women, to help them realize that if they are attacked or abused they can do something about it. My motto is "don't do nothing."

PERSPECTIVES

When one door of happiness closes, another opens, but often we look so long at the closed door that we do not see the one that has been opened for us.
Helen Keller

Perspectives

This chapter contains brief personal thoughts, insights, and opinions, of some highly-recognized women in the martial arts, on what it means to be a female martial artist.

1. Who is the martial arts woman to you?

DANA STAMOS: Women who train seriously in the martial arts have a special strength and determination. They are different from their peers because hard physical and mental training develops an inner strength that is not normally developed in day-to-day life.

Martial arts students learn discipline, focus, and something not often learned early in life, the ability to withstand pain without fear. Martial arts teach balance, and the ability to turn off the outside world while you train. This is very difficult for me. These abilities are helpful in everything that you do.

Female martial artists who teach are generally high achievers, disciplined, and willing to give their all to their students. They must have discernment, know when to push a student beyond his physical limits, and build emotional strength in their students.

KRISTEN MILLER: I believe the martial arts woman is strong, confident, and a leader. She lives her life being confident in who she is, but at the same time always works to make herself better than she was yesterday.

MICHELLE MANU: The martial arts woman is any woman who actively trains in martial arts, regardless of style. This group is comprised of different ethnicities, nationalities, economic, social, and academic backgrounds. They have varying body styles, output, capabilities, talents and gifts.

The martial arts woman actively seeks self-awareness and self-evolutionary practices that she applies to her life. She can be a woman who teaches in a commercial, traditional, or sport martial arts school. She may study at an MMA gym, or in the garage of a master, or in an elemental training setting. A martial arts woman is any woman on the spectrum who wants to challenge herself to be more.

These principles include incorporating her intention and purpose for her martial art training into her physical, emotional, mental, spiritual, and relational realms of her being. A martial art woman is a woman who studies martial arts on her path to self-mastery.

2. How is a female martial artist "empowered?"

DANA STAMOS: You must develop mental strength, as well as physical strength, to excel in your martial arts training. In general, men already have a penchant for fighting because their desire is to protect. Women, on the other hand, are nurturers, and it can be difficult for them to use aggression, even when it is necessary.

We must let go of who we are, and do what our instructors tell us to do. Next, we must learn to respond to an attack. Then, we must adapt to control the response, depending on the intent of the aggressor.

I often felt out of control when going up against the bigger guys with whom I worked out. Instead of using my head, or using my opponent's strength against him, I tried to muscle my way through. There is a lot of thought that goes into the techniques used in fighting systems, and it takes time to learn how to think and react quickly, and use the best technique for that situation.

KRISTEN MILLER: I believe a female martial artist becomes empowered though the martial arts by pushing herself beyond her own limits, and always taking things to the next level. Martial arts teach you how to commit to something and persevere. That is something that you can take out of the dojo and into your personal life.

Martial arts also teach you to be physically and mentally strong and to be always prepared. When you have a strong body and a strong mind, you carry yourself differently. You believe in your ability to get through any situation.

MICHELLE MANU: A female martial artist becomes empowered when the unseen becomes seen, or when all things internal become an outward expression. We manifest this power into self-confidence and perseverance into all aspects of life.

All things start and end with Self (not little self, but big Self.) Little self is the woman that hides behind the appearance of perfect in her manners, dojo etiquette, katas, and point fighting. She is a perfect lady in her communications, and the style expected of her. Big Self is little self, but with a spiritual temperature of where she is in life, not just martial arts.

Out of this spiritual tempering and honest self-awareness, this courageous martial arts woman clears her path to become whom she chooses to be. She has clear and purposeful intent. She helps others with integrity, persistence, honesty, and good intent. In time, she learns to apply those virtues to herself.

During this internal Self-time, this courageous woman evaluates her choices, and decides what needs to be let go in her private life and in the dojo. She also decides on what she will focus and pursue. Past spiritual pains from a person, place, or event need to be examined, felt, and forgiven (others and self). She must vow to adopt newer and more beneficial ways of handling life.

This internal "weeding of the garden" is the core and relentless fire of true self-empowerment. She no longer needs to feel like a victim of circumstance, as she renews every time she makes a creative choice. Without this, she will never reach her potential or purpose during her time here on earth. Through empowerment, this uncompromising spirit is the beginning of mastery over self, transitioning into Self. This is the ultimate goal, male or female, through martial arts.

3. Does a woman compromise her femininity in martial arts?

DANA STAMOS: Women in the martial arts do not need to be more aggressive or less feminine, but they do need to work on physical strength and stamina. Martial arts are about understanding body mechanics and using them to your benefit. This comes with getting the proper training.

KRISTEN MILLER: I do not believe women compromise their femininity. I believe it is beautiful and attractive to be strong physically as well as mentally. I believe it is feminine to be a strong woman.

4. What are your thoughts about fighting or sparring?

DANA STAMOS: Sparring is important in everyday training for men and women, not just in tournaments. I often sparred with women who were much smaller than I was, and I did not have to use proper technique. Other times, I sparred with men bigger and heavier who pounded on me just to prove a point. Neither situation was productive.

A balance needs to discovered in sparring. It is the responsibility of a good instructor guides and allows the student to grow and stretch through what sparring offers.

KRISTEN MILLER: I had some issues to overcome with sparring. It has not always been my favorite part of the martial arts. It is not fun if you do not have the right training partners. I do not consider myself a fighter. It can be intimidating if you are the only female, especially if you are the smallest one in the class.

I only sparred because it was required. I would do it because I knew it would make me a better martial artist, but I did not always enjoy it. I would say that has changed over the years. I do not look at it the same way anymore. Now I see it as an opportunity to learn, and I ask myself how would I counter a real-life situation, or avoid being in a bad situation in the first place.

MICHELLE MANU: In the Kaihewalu Lua we fight on cement, wear shoes, and rarely wear gloves or headgear (which looks like a hockey mask). If we do, we wear the fingerless, slightly padded gloves, so we can still do the mano (shark) and popoki (cat) face and skin bites when we are fighting.

It is not point fighting; it is continuous. Olohe can also call a couple more guys into the fight so it ends up being two against one or three against one.

As the only woman in about 35 years to be a first-generation black belt in the Lua Halau O Kaihewalu, I cannot stress how important it was to be better than my male koa haumanas (warrior students). First was quickness. I must get out of the line of fire, and fire something immediately before they retract what they sent to me.

Secondly was mana (power). I am 5'7" and between 140-150 pounds at any time. I needed to develop my mana. I needed to ignore what was programmed into me since I was young. Women learn to keep men out of their space, act lady-like, not make a scene, and just deal with issues quietly. When I changed that programming, I could keep my bones and rib cage intact. I would need to be uncomfortable to develop my "in-fighting", which means that my opponent is literally a couple inches from me until I move in and make him part of my body.

Women have been misled. They are so strong on the inside. They will defend how they train. They will age how they maintain. My fellow black belts did me a favor by shooting straight for my face at real speed. If they did not, I would have learned nothing from my training. I could have gone to kickboxing aerobics for that.

Women need to move past the uncomfortableness of having someone in their space and develop true power. Even when I did that, it did not exempt me from a broken rib, baseball-sized hematoma, fractured hip, multiple breaks, and more.

Next, is fear (and that instinctive eye blink or flurry). Fear cannot live when you fully commit to an endeavor. Once you commit, you are responsible for effort, not outcome. This applies to all things in life. To think you can control outcomes is silly as there are many people and karmic factors in play always.

In my first eight years of training, I realized that no one would ever come to my rescue. Out on the street or in a vulnerable situation, I cannot rely on anyone but myself.

My awareness, safety, and survival are solely my kuleana (responsibility). There is no knight in shining armor on a white horse that is going to come riding into the alley if I get jumped by a couple of guys. Life is not a Disney movie, where the princess or unfairly treated servant, needs rescuing. I will always rescue myself.

How you train, whether on the street or in the dojo, is similar to how you will react to a real-life situation. Flight, fight, or freeze. Which one will you choose before an incident occurs? If you have not trained for these situations, or you have not vowed that you will fight until you have no breath left in you, it is most likely you may not survive.

Decide now that you will fight and get away, even if you are hurt and can see, smell, and feel your blood. I can sum my message up in these truths: fight, get away, and have no fear.

"If we are going to survive this, you need to remember, fear is not real. It is a product of the thoughts you create. Now do not misunderstand me; danger is very real. But fear is a choice." Will Smith in *After Earth*

JENNY SIKORA: The fact that I´m able to fight, protect, and take care of myself as a woman is because of my martial art training and self-defense classes. They make me feel more independent, powerful, safe, secure, and free.

5. Why do women quit martial arts?

DANA STAMOS: All aspects of the martial arts require that you stay in shape and train consistently. This takes time and effort. There are two different sides to martial arts. The sport side of martial arts is when you enjoy competing in forms and sparring. The "martial" side of martial arts is when you are preparing for combat and learn to be a warrior.

Like anything worthwhile, you need to have a desire to succeed. There are more men in the martial arts just because that they are "martial." Often martial arts are a course of protection versus lifelong training for a woman.

Some women love training, and continue, while others learn what they need at the time, then move on. When I was a child I wanted to practice martial arts with my brother, but in those days, girls were not practicing the arts. I began as an adult when I enrolled my children in Tang Soo Do.

KRISTEN MILLER: I think there are varying reasons why women quit. I know that some moms leave because they put their family first. They feel as if they did not have the time to take for themselves. I do not see that happen as much with men.

MICHELLE MANU: I am not sure why some women quit. I do not think it is always gender specific, because I have seen many men come and go in the Halau. From personal experience, teaching women can be extremely challenging. Besides not knowing their worth, and rarely putting their desires first (this includes their training), any insignificant life event seems to derail their consistent attendance or home study. Life happens.

The other issue with which I have difficulty understanding is the continued cry for self-defense, yet no one signs up or attends when it is scheduled. It boggles my sensibilities. My sister, a former psychologist, says that when she hears "self-defense," she begins to laugh as if it is a stand-up comedic act. She says, "Honestly Michelle, I would rather have a root canal than attend a self-defense workshop. What a waste of time." This surprises me because she has four daughters.

6. How does martial arts affect your motherhood?

DANA STAMOS: I began martial arts in my mid-thirties with my children. Start you children in martial arts when they are young to prevent them from bullies in the future. Do not let them quit before they have reaped the benefits of the martial arts, including discipline, focus, and confidence. A child with these traits will not show up in the bully's radar. Bullies choose children without those traits.

KRISTEN MILLER: I believe martial arts make me a better mother. When I go to class, I am showing my girls it is important to make time for yourself. I show them that it is important to keep yourself strong, and your health should be a priority.

I like the fact that they have seen me spar and look at me as a strong person who can stick up for myself. My two daughters, ages 10 and 12, have been training since they were 2 and ½ years old. They are exposed to the 5 principles of being a black belt, including courtesy, integrity, perseverance, self-control, and indomitable spirit. They know this is not just something about which we talk. We try to make ourselves better than we were yesterday, and this is how we live our lives.

MICHELLE MANU: I am a mother and a recent grandmother of twin grand boys. My daughter practiced more than three years of extreme Lua training starting when she was 11. Because of her real-life training, I never have a moment of worry about her taking care of herself. This provides me with tremendous peace of mind in day-to-day, emergency, and survival situations.

We have always had a code word for when we are in public. If I said it or wrote it, she knew to be hyper-aware and to position herself in between me and the problem, person, or event. I know she will train her boys in the same way.

JENNY SIKORA: Based on my experiences of being a stepmother to an 11-year-old girl, I've found the martial arts and warrior lifestyle philosophy to be a great guidance. I use these philosophies to teach and prepare my stepdaughter to make the right decisions in her life. This will help her grow up to be an independent, strong, and caring woman later in her life, with good values and principles.

The fact that I can share my insights with her and teach her about self-defense is very important to me.

JACKIE BRADBURY: I was a martial art mom long before I became a martial artist myself. We wanted to enroll our oldest daughter in the martial arts as soon as we were able. My daughter is a very sweet, highly empathetic kid who is the type of personality who would allow other kids to run roughshod over her. We wanted her to try martial arts to learn how to stand up for herself. It worked. She is now a strong, self-confident person, and nobody's doormat.

My younger daughter, however, has a different problem. Her view of the world is very self-oriented, and she is not naturally sensitive to the feelings of other people. For her, we hoped that martial art training would connect her to a world bigger than herself. We wanted her to learn how to be more naturally empathetic, and understand how her behavior affects those around her. We also wanted her to establish more discipline that is personal.

Martial arts are a natural part of our entire family's life, so I do not know what kind of mom I would be without it. Being an instructor of both children and adults teaches me patience. I can view my kids with more objectivity because of it.

I am sure I still worry as much as any other mom. Maybe I worry more because I am more aware as to what can go wrong, thanks to my training in self-defense. I fight hard against my "helicopter parent" tendencies! I do not believe that over-sheltering children is good for them, even though my instinct says to wrap them in bubble wrap and keep them behind a 10-foot-tall concrete fence so nobody can hurt them.

7. Have you had any personal obstacles or challenges to overcome that you used a "martial art mindset?"

DANA STAMOS: I was born with monocular vision. This means I see out of one eye at a time and have no depth perception. This is not a problem with my eyes, but rather with how the right and left side of my brain work together with perceptions in things like math, or music. Later in life, I was in an accident that also affected my short-term memory.

Martial arts help with all these things. You must be able to use both the right and left sides of the brain together to perform techniques. They affect how you memorize kata, discover the "fight" in the kata, and how you use the techniques as you move in and out of the kata.

When practicing sparring, you should know where your opponent is always. Then, you must plan your strikes to the most effective points so they work. Because of my monocular vision, these things were very difficult for me, but the longer I trained the easier they became.

KRISTEN MILLER: I have used my martial art mindset to overcome many personal obstacles. Perseverance has helped me get through times when I have felt like giving up. It taught me to be calm, breathe, and keep my head clear.

Years ago, we were in a bad car accident. A drunk driver hit us. My 6-year daughter was badly injured. She had thirteen fractures in her face, two teeth knocked out and a small laceration on her face. We were in the ER, and my husband and I were very scared. Even though I was terrified for my daughter, I could stay calm for her. I believe this is just one example of how, at times like this, martial arts training keeps you calm and focused under extreme pressure.

MICHELLE MANU: Not everyone views or approaches life the same way, and they should not. Sometimes, we forget that some people live by a lesser set of rules, self-awareness, conscience, or self-governing, ethical standards. Generally, there is an unwritten code between martial artists, regardless of what art they study. Not everyone should expect the martial mindset. Expecting a non-martial artist to display and live by martial virtues will lead to unnecessary disappointment. Then again, not all "martial artists" live by this code, either.

JENNY SIKORA: The martial art and warrior lifestyle has a distinct philosophy that has provided me with guidance, wisdom and awareness in life. I feel prepared to overcome every single obstacle that comes my direction, without ever wanting to give up.

Through this lifestyle, I have been able to find something about which to be grateful every single day. Even on a bad day, I am still able to smile because I'm proud of the way that I'm handling life.

8. When should a martial arts woman be "savage?"

DANA STAMOS: We never need to be a savage, but we do have to use the right amount of force to get the job done. We cannot be afraid to protect others or ourselves.

Being savage means being out of control, and the more we train the less "out of control" we are. Martial arts techniques and training allows us to use the right technique and force when needed. We are in control and deadly, but not savage.

KRISTEN MILLER: I believe a martial arts woman needs to be savage when she is fighting. That can be during sparring or simply when working out. Sometimes she must reveal her savage side and allow it to emerge through the challenge in fighting, and because her belief system may be challenged.

9. How are female martial artists different from male martial artists?

DANA STAMOS: We are all different from each other in every way. Our backgrounds will affect who we are, and how we respond. Our height, weight and flexibility will determine how we move. Our strength and ability to flow will affect our techniques.

As I said in a previous response, men are protective by nature, while women are nurturing by nature. In this regard, a woman may have to work a little harder on her ability to use the right amount of force, but it is nothing she cannot do. There is usually body weight, height, and muscle mass differences, but women can learn to use these things to her advantage. The key is to find the right instructor.

KRISTEN MILLER: I believe that women do not have the egos that most men have. I believe that a woman in the martial arts is usually the minority, and that creates a special bond. I feel women try to support each other in different ways than men do. Since we cannot always use our strength, it becomes more of a mental challenge.

JENNY SIKORA: The biggest difference between women and men, when it comes to martial arts and the warrior lifestyle, is the reasons behind their decisions and motivation to practice martial arts in the first place.

10. In what way are women evolving in the arts/breaking stereotypes?

DANA STAMOS: In life, we want to be the best we can be, male or female. We all feel that we have a certain calling, and we should not feel the need to outdo others at anything. It is more important to exceed our own expectations and grow constantly and consistently.

I believe that men and women are stronger together than they are apart. They are different, but complement one another. A woman warrior can still be nurturing and feminine, and use logic and technique just as effectively as any man. The truth is, none of us will always be the most effective in every situation, and we must learn to let our egos go to be as effective as possible.

We need to celebrate our differences and work in tandem, so we can all find success. We cannot allow stereotypes that hold us back. Our differences make us unique.

KRISTEN MILLER: I have trained for the past 18 years. I see more young girls and female adults training now. I remember training at my old school and thinking, please let there be another girl in class! At my school, about 50% of our students are female.

I was speaking to another school owner today who said 60% of his students were female, and his demo team was predominantly female.

MICHELLE MANU: An amazing evolution is happening. I witness it every day. I notice it the most when I am hired to teach a seminar or workshop as a guest instructor. The evolution begins the moment I they introduce me and I walk onto the floor or mat.

As I begin speaking, there are unmistakable facial expressions from certain men. I can almost hear them saying, "What is this woman going to show me that I don't already know? Great, a couple of hours of katas? Oh, come on. On the street, what could she possibly do to me?"

I make sure I use these very men in demonstrations, or deliberately correct them when I am walking around. They are the same men who later slyly line up after the workshop to speak with me. They usually finally abandon their biases and accept me, and genuinely want to know more about the Lua and Hula, the Hawaiian warrior ways.

These amazing men ultimately become my biggest advocates and relentless supporters. There are high leaps made in the world. Powerful women of all ages are emerging, and men and women finally accept them.

11. How does your martial art affect your relationships/marriage?

KRISTEN MILLER: I think martial arts help me in every one of my relationships. When I am training regularly, I know I feel better, and I am happier. If I am happy, stronger both physically and mentally, and have less stress in my life, I feel I am at my best.

If I am at my best, I have more to give. Martial arts have helped me to keep calm, centered, and positive. I believe we can spread this contagious energy. I want to surround myself with those kinds of people.

MICHELLE MANU: When I was married for 12 years, my husband really did not have an opinion. For the subsequent 8 years, I did not date while I raised my daughter. I focused on her, my Lua training, working, and earning additional academic degrees.

I slowly started dating four years ago, and I do not really talk much about the details of being a martial artist. I prefer not talking about it, because it is for me alone. I have never dated a martial artist. Any man that I choose to date must understand, and not provoke, diminish, or disrespect, my training or teaching. I am involved in many martial art related projects.

At times, it seems that men see dating me as a conquest. Whenever I feel that sort of energy, I make it known through my actions that I am not the answer. Acquiring me will not enhance their masculinity, nor will I serve as the new fancy car for them to make an entrance.

JENNY SIKORA: Back when I used to date, my lifestyle and philosophy scared some men because I was so independent and confident. In the end, however, it gained me their respect.

The martial arts and the warrior lifestyle philosophy reminded me what the important qualities are in a man, such as integrity, intelligence, manners and behavior. Instead of choosing men based on their appearance, I base it on these things.

Our greatest weakness lies in giving up. The most certain way to succeed is always to try just one more time.
Thomas A. Edison

CONCLUSION

Martial art women are difficult to define or categorize, but they share many similar beliefs, attitudes, and experiences. Femininity, motherhood, love, courage, positivity, bravery, and warriorship, are some of the characteristics that make them so unique and spirited.

When writing this book, I never realized that the breadth of so many intriguing and unique experiences would reveal. Suddenly, I was not the only martial art woman who had experienced, braved, and battled difficult and powerful personal journeys. I no longer felt like my stories were not worth telling. I was encouraged and renewed by the words of the other contributors. Before my eyes, the aura and energy of the female martial artist unfolded.

My goal in this book, and in my ongoing outreach, is to be the voice of the martial art woman. The contributors to this book embody a true and unique martial art spirit. They selflessly revealed their most personal selves, and shared their truths about powerful living and thinking through martial arts. Their stories, insights, and journeys are meaningful on so many different levels.

A story, reflection, or insight within these pages will guide you, no matter where you are in your own life. No longer must you feel alone or too scared to try, take a risk, or move ahead with your dreams. The importance of these stories is not about how they influence me, but how they influence you.

After reading this book, you should have a better understanding of the significance of the martial art woman. You should begin to see your life in a new light and realize your own abilities to be a magnificent warrior. You can meet every battle head on with persistence, perseverance, and positivity.

If the martial arts woman represents anything, it is that her mind, body, and spirit affect the world in a uniquely womanly way. Her training rivals that of a man, but her perspective is different. Who knows what the future holds? Where will she go from here? How will the martial arts woman thrive and change?

I cannot answer any of those questions, but I know one thing for sure. Whatever happens, and however she evolves, the martial arts woman will always contribute a significant chapter to the world of martial arts. Now I have told some of her stories, and her character and bravery is established.

I wrote this book to explore the soul of the martial arts woman, to unearth her stagnant voice, and to clarify how she humbly and consistently makes a difference through her practice and application of martial arts. My sincere wish is that you cultivate your own powerful and fulfilling life journey by applying the perspectives, insights, psyche, and spirit of the martial arts woman to your life.

Andrea Harkins
About the Author

Andrea Harkins, also known as The Martial Arts Woman, is a martial artist, instructor, motivator, blogger, speaker, published author, and life coach. She strives to share her martial art vision and positivity, through black belt concepts and life lessons, as an outreach to others.

Andrea has been training in the martial arts since 1989. She continues to teach, often for free, to mentor children and adults in martial arts. She and her family have been teaching their own martial art program at a community YMCA for the past seven years for youth, teens, and adults.

To ignite her passion, and share her vision, Andrea began writing her blog, www.themartialartswoman.com several years ago, which is a popular and candid account of martial arts and life. Her life coaching and motivational speaking information is available at www.andreaharkins.com.

Andrea eventually became recognized for her writing and was invited to be a columnist for such prestigious magazines as *Think Positive Magazine, MASUCCESS, The World Martial Arts Magazine, Conflict Manager, Martial Art Guardian (UK), Martial Arts Illustrated (UK), Martial Arts Business* (Australia), as well as the newspaper, *The Parrish Village News.*

She has been interviewed by *Martial Arts Nation Podcast, Martial Thoughts, Warrior Radio, Warriorcast, The Dynamic Dojo Radio Show, Modern Combat Masters Radio Show, Whistlekick Martial Arts Radio, Sisters in Harmony, Life is a Marathon,* and *Isshinryu Today.* In 2015 she was touted as a rising star by the *World Martial Arts Magazine,* and featured in *Martial Arts Illustrated UK* in 2016. In late 2016, she was on the cover of the *World Martial Arts Magazine* in recognition for her positivity through martial arts mission.

Andrea's positivity, martial art experiences, and writing have captured the attention of thousands of friends, fans, and followers, who are motivated and inspired by her succinct and poignant views on martial arts and life.

Please Take a Couple of Minutes to Review
The Martial Arts Woman!

Reader reviews are very important to authors in today's fast-paced world and I value your opinion. Reviews are the lifeblood of the author. Posting a quick review on Amazon and on Facebook, and other social media, really helps authors out.

If you have enjoyed *The Martial Arts Woman*, please consider taking just a couple of minutes and reviewing it on Amazon and on your social media pages. Also, please tell your friends about *The Martial Arts Woman*. I would sincerely appreciate it.

Thank you!

Andrea Harkins

Made in the USA
Middletown, DE
19 December 2025

25270518R00126